FIRE
BEARER

F I R E
BEARER

Evoking a Priestly Humanity

MICHAEL DWINELL

TRIUMPH™ BOOKS
Liguori, Missouri

Published by Triumph™ Books
Liguori, Missouri
An Imprint of Liguori Publications

The author wishes to thank the staff and faculty of Fairfax University for their generous support of the work and ideas that developed into this book.

Library of Congress Cataloging-in-Publication Data

Dwinell, Michael
   Fire bearer : evoking a priestly humanity / Michael Dwinell. — 1st ed.
     p. cm.
   Includes bibliographical references
   ISBN 0-89243-531-3 : $16.95
   1. Priesthood—Meditations. 2. Clergy—Office—Meditations.
   3. Catholic Church—Clergy–Religious life—Meditations. I. Title.
BX1912.5.D95 1993
242′.692—dc20   92-43418
                                               CIP

Printed in the United States of America

First Edition

Dedication

This book is for those who, not by their own choosing, have been touched in their mothers' womb with the divine madness and, therefore, have no choice but to struggle with that irrefutable core fact for the entirety of their lives.

I write in loving gratitude for the courage of the women and men I have known, ordained and not ordained, who have struggled with their vocation to be priest. When all is said and done, it is the example and modeling by other human beings of courage and faithfulness that has made the essential difference. Individual human lives struggling with integrity and vocation are sacramental; flesh, bodies, brain cells, blood, and bones are messengers of grace.

I want to remember especially and express my deepest gratitude for Priest and Bishop, the Rt. Rev. Frederick B. Wolf, who struggled so fiercely and so openly with his vocation that he was a testament of priestly vulnerability for me and for many, a man both gifted and burdened with a never-ending well of compassion.

CONTENTS

— ◊ —

FORTY DAYS

IN THE TEMPLE

CRUCIFIXION, RESURRECTION

PREFACE

THE BOOK is arranged in twenty-three self-contained meditations. Each meditation has both an expository section and one or more narratives that, hopefully, give voice to the more theoretical language of the expository section. The book can be read either in one sitting or used as a series of ongoing meditations, one at a time.

At the end of the narrative section of each meditation, the reader is invited to add his or her own images or thoughts and narratives. In each meditation, the connection between the expository section and the narrative section is often not literal or obvious but associational and imaginal, which is, of course, at the heart of the nature of priest. The reader is asked to recall that our faith is given to us not primarily through theory but rather through narrative — the Great Story, and all the stories therein.

Unless otherwise indicated, all narratives are written by Michael Dwinell. Any narrative not written by Michael Dwinell is indicated by the name of its author, unless the author wishes to remain anonymous. All narratives are used with permission.

INTRODUCTION

WHEN I WAS ORDAINED first deacon, and then priest, I knew one thing for sure: I did not know what I was doing. While in the parish ministry, I was aware of responding to myriad expectations that assaulted me from all directions. They came from parishioners, other clergy, lay people outside the parish, my family, the Bishop. There were, of course, all my own internal expectations, chief among them that I could fill everyone else's expectations. All this kept me very busy and flooded me with anxiety. None of it had anything to do with being a priest.

I had been trained to be a pastor, a teacher, an administrator, a professional, a preacher, even sometimes a prophet; but I had no idea what it was to be priest. No one had ever taught me that. I felt inadequate because I assumed all other priests, in some secret and mysterious way, already had learned how to be priest; I had been left out.

Even though I knew what I was supposed to be doing to fulfill the conventional expectations of parish ministry, and even though I was doing it competently and satisfactorily, I was not yet being priest. I felt like a chameleon. A great deal of energy and time was spent trying to sort out the requests, the demands, the assumptions, and the expectations coming both from within as well as from parishioners. I tried saying no, because I felt the expectations weren't right, but I had no idea with what to replace them. What in God's name was I supposed to say yes to? I spent *myself* trying to reduce the sense of prostitution and self-betrayal to an acceptable minimum.

During this time, I certainly didn't want anyone evaluating or peering too closely at my ministry; just beneath the surface lay a horrible sense of fraud. I wasn't doing what I was supposed to be doing. I wasn't being faithful. I was selling out. Worst of all, while feeling totally helpless and lost, I was actually a willing perpetrator — working harder, putting in longer hours, trying to do more and more — despite an increasing sense of insecurity, inadequacy, and sinfulness.

It was not until more recently, after much reflection and struggle, I discovered the images and expectations of what it is to be priest generated not from without but from deep within me. Finally, I can say a loud and clear NO to external demands and expectations because I have a sense of what to say yes to; I have something else to offer from inside which feels strong and good and honest and faithful. Finally, I am not ashamed to have others look at my ministry.

In dialogue with others, ordained or in the process of becoming ordained to priesthood, and in talks with those who are baptismally consecrated or likewise claimed, I have discovered that "the call" most often comes very early in a person's life, perhaps even before birth. Vocation is real. Those who are called assert that they know it from their first moment of awareness, perhaps at two or three years of age. They know that they have been set apart, called, set in the center. They know that they have been given special capacity to be aware, to listen for the heavenly music, to look beneath the surface for the meaning of all things.

Quite often, when an infant is touched by the divine madness, that call is experienced as a recurring set of images — dream or nightmare. It is without words, without theological or religious understanding, but imaginally, utterly clear, haunting, and formative.

This sense of being set beyond normal, of knowing there is more, and of being called is a constant summoning. Those thus summoned often spend the first half of their life building an ego structure, a sense of identity strong enough to carry the truths of vocation they discovered laid upon them at the earliest moments of their existence. Usually at the same time, immense amounts of psychological energy are spent attempting to avoid, deny, or prove false those early revelations.

As one reaches adulthood, there is a disparity between who one *tells* the world he or she is, and who one secretly *knows* he or she is and is to become. This disparity is experienced as shame, cowardice, self-hatred, unfaithfulness. When people later in life finally begin to say yes to the being they most certainly sensed they were in their early years, relief and joy displace shame and fear. Being priest is a turning toward home, a daring by the grace of God to finally be faithful to the "who" one was created to be.

The hope of these meditations, then, is to lift up the image of priest as one would elevate a diamond, then to walk around the elevated jewel discerning in how many ways the image of priest might be seen and revealing in how many ways we might find ourselves reflected in that image. Priest is a rich, many-faceted mystery in which we are all drenched.

If we as people and a species do not recover the sense of mystery of priest, our extinction is assured. Not the stereotypes of priest: pastor, minister, rector; rather, the archetype of priest itself must be revisioned. At the heart of the jewel of archetypal priest is transformation; and we as a species are on the threshold of transformation, the threshold of the evolution of consciousness, the threshold of transformation or extinction. If we are not able to evolve, to enter into transformation, we will surely do ourselves in, for we cannot go on as we are. There can be no evolutionary transformation without knowing priest, for only by knowing priest, and the priest gift of transformation, can we believe that there is real hope. Priest is hope. Without knowing priest, we have no choice but to settle for the mediocrity of extinction.

People who live without the vocation of priest (agent of transformation) have at the end nothing left but the pursuit of survival. Life has no meaning beyond that. We then, individually and collectively, become reduced to predators one upon the other, greed becomes elevated as a virtue, and survival becomes dubious.

Only if we believe that there is more, that there are additional realities beyond our "normal," will we contest extinction. That knowing of "the more" is witnessed to and proclaimed by the mere presence of priest. Without the recollecting of priest, we are already sealed in the tombs of our own paltry reality.

Priest is not owned or possessed by any particular denomination or church or Christianity or any religion. Rather, it is an archetypal energy given to each and all by God. It is a universal gift and cannot be controlled or owned by any particular organization or group. It is, therefore, an essential mystical gift for all creation.

Not only is priest an essential mystery for all of us, but also a mystery for each of us. Of all the magnificent jewels in each of our royal crowns, priest is the gem that returns the most splendor. Without this cardinal centerpiece, the crown is curiously irrelevant, no matter how ornate. To be priest is to be faithful, faithful to the Lord of transformation. Each of us is created to be an agent of transformation — priest, ordained or not.

Since all of us are called to faithfulness, we can say that the journey of priest toward faithfulness is essentially everybody's journey. Likewise, the vocation of the ordained priest is vocation, i.e., the calling into consciousness of every person to the vocation of becoming an agent of transformation.

I offer this collection of images to my brothers and sisters who have been burnt by divine madness, hoping the offering might excite and provoke the wealth of images within and thus be for them nourishment, balm, and salvation from fraudulent obscenity.

Only when our ministries are shaped by the power of images and metaphors that spring up from the deepest recesses of our own souls, are we able to know who and what is priest.

CREATION

PRIEST AS CALLED*

Dear Duncan,

Many, many months ago you wrote me in your loving way from England, speaking from your "Quaker" self, and asked me, "What on earth has moved you to write a book about being priest?"

That question has been roaming about within me all this time, and I now finally feel ready to answer.

It has become clear to me that a human being cannot become fully human, fully whole, fully real, fully completed, unless he is both moving into and living out of his priestliness. That is to say, unless he is consciously and volitionally seeking to live his life as an agent of transformation. That is the vocation to which we are all essentially called. Regardless of what else we may do with our lives, if the priest part is absent, not only are we less than complete but also we regress and degrade into predatory subhumanness. In fact, I would go as far as to say if we — all of us — do not allow

---

*A Letter to My Brother.

ourselves to be claimed by the vocation of priesthood, we will not survive as a species.

Two biblical images come to mind. The first is the story of Jesus and the resuscitation from death of his friend Lazarus.

Remember that when Jesus is told that Lazarus is ill and dying, he consciously and pointedly makes the decision to delay his arrival by two days, thus guaranteeing that Lazarus's illness would be fatal. When Jesus finally does arrive, the two sisters of Lazarus rage at him for not coming to rescue Lazarus when he first heard of the illness. Recall also that Jesus goes before the place where Lazarus's body lies and calls to him, "Come out"; the dead man comes back to life.

Reflecting on this passage, we must simultaneously remember that it is Jesus who says that we are his sisters and his brothers. It is Jesus who calls us his disciples. It is Jesus who says, "I am in you and you are in me." It is Jesus who says to us, "You shall do as I have done and greater things still."

Most of us would never presume to identify with Jesus in any of the Gospel stories. I think we would be even more reluctant, perhaps even terrified, to identify with Lazarus, to be the one receiving such intense, life-giving energy. But by Jesus' own words, we must identify with him in this story of Lazarus. I believe we are called by Jesus himself into a priestly humanity that has both the inner authority to decide to delay — to let things die that need to die — and the power to call out and revive that which has been dead. Even beyond receiving the energy of God, we must also, and more importantly, become transmitters — priests.

The second biblical image is about what happens to us when we, faithful to our vocation of priestliness, become agents of transformation. You remember that Shadrach, Meshach, and Abednego refused to relinquish their standpoint, their conviction in *Yahweh* in the face of Nebuchadnezzar's command that they worship *his* gods. Nebuchadnezzar is enraged by their refusal and has them thrown into a blazing furnace so hot that it consumes some of the attendants who built the fire. And yet, when Nebuchadnezzar looks into the flames, he sees Shadrach, Meshach, and Abednego walking about, unconsumed, unharmed, and accompanied by a mysterious fourth presence.

I believe that when we are faithful to our priestly vocation, we stand in the flames of our own fires — a public fire, for all to see, that does not consume us and a fire in which we are accompanied by the "holy other" who walks with us. If we are not faithful to our vocation, I believe that the fire remains within, hidden away inside where it does consume us and where we thus walk unaccompanied and self-alienated.

So priesthood is everybody's destiny, everybody's vocation. Without it we are not human, and with it we are enabled to stand, unconsumed and walking with the holy one, within our own fires. The single most compassionate act we can perform is to hold each other accountable to our priesthood.

Much love,
Michael

Fire Bearing in the Imagination

A 35-year old woman had the following dream as a child. It recurred often and she experienced it as a nightmare.

> I am standing at the door of a huge fire, like a furnace. Everything is ablaze. There is a dark figure standing next to me. I cannot see his face. People bring me children and infants. They defecate on me and I know I must throw them into the fire, one at a time. The dark presence beside me insists that I must do this.

Both as a child and as an adult, she experienced this dream horrifically. She was sure it was revealing her as an evil, evil person. Initially she thought it was her brothers and sisters she was throwing into the fire, and later she thought it was anyone with whom she came in contact. She has carried that image of herself as a wicked, sadistic, evil murderess for years and years.

When it was suggested to her that perhaps the images of this dream were "just right" and might be the images of her vocation, she was stunned, shocked, and even more terrified.

She was asked what she did professionally. She said, "I am a teacher of little children." She was then asked, "What do you teach them?" "I'm supposed to teach them health," she said. Finally she was asked, "What do you really teach them?" "I try to show them the meaning of the world. I try to fire up their imaginations. I try to show them life. I try to speak to their souls."

Then she looked up, and said, "Oh, my God! The dream really is about teaching, about my work, isn't it?" And she wept and wept and wept, great sobbing tears of relief.

Then she started to laugh with peals of delight, "And the kids often shit all over me for doing this!"

She saw that she was indeed called to be a person to whom people brought children, and it is her job to throw them into the fire, and that the dark presence standing beside her is not Satan but God.

A Second Priest's Dream

She dreamed that she was in front of the man who is her companion, dearest friend, and lover. He was sitting on the floor with his knees drawn up before him. He was requesting that she pour flammable fluid all over his body and ignite it. He was telling her that this was a necessary process to change his skin and his hair. So she found lighter fluid, soaked him down, and with a match set it off to watch his skin, his hair, and his face burn and change.

This is a dream of a young woman studying to be an acupuncturist. She is wrestling with fear and trepidation about the power and authority of her role in the lives of those who come to her for her help and ask intervention. She is more than ambivalent about her power and authority.

Notice that once she touches the lighter fluid, the process of transformation takes off by itself with unknown and awesome consequences.

This role as agent of transformation, this awesome and terrifying function of being able to initiate the process of incredibly painful and marvelous transformation in another, is the vocation of each and every one of us.

We are all called to set each other on fire.

PRIEST AS SEEING

TO LOOK at priest means to see — to see ourselves, seeing; to know ourselves as creatures who are capable of seeing. That which sees is seen. The primary activity of the human psyche is to image, to imagine. What we respond to when we see is the image in our own mind of what is seen, so that in looking, it is the one who sees who is provoked. To see priest is to be profoundly provoked. Priest may be the most provocative of all images. To be priest is, first, to know the vitality of all images. To be priest is first to know the vitality of the human psyche in the act of seeing, imaging, and projecting. The mystery of priest is not just that priest is mystery, but that priest arouses the deepest sense of mystery in each person who beholds priest. The image of priest arouses priest within. The image of priest arouses within no less than the deepest of all mystery.

The Awakening

When as a visiting clergy I enter a church to conduct a service for a congregation that I have never seen, it

is impossible not to be incredibly aware of the *seeing*
going on. All eyes are upon me, and if there are a hundred people in the congregation, I can literally feel a
hundred different images being projected upon me, as
if something living were flung upon my body and were
sticking to me. I know that for each of the people in
the congregation the experience of this new priest is
unique and different. The curiosity and the need to see
is intense, and whether what they see is *good* or *bad*, it
is at least not neutral. The deepest values and emotions
are stirred. Whether they like what they see or don't
like what they see, they are engaged in the mystery of
seeing and imaging. They are awake.

The Reflection

In the afternoon following my ordination, I left the
cathedral and walked with my friends along the side-
walks of the city streets. Glancing into the window of
a large department store, I saw a man dressed in a
suit and wearing a clerical collar. I was startled, and
I jumped and said, 'Oh, my God, there is a priest!' It
was my own reflection in the store window.

PRIEST AS MATTER

SEVERAL BILLIONS of years ago, energy transformed itself into matter. There is nothing about energy that makes its transformation into matter necessary, but it happened, and energy and matter have inner-penetrated ever since. Over time, matter has become self-organizing and self-conscious. Likewise, there is nothing in matter that would compel it to become self-organizing and self-conscious life, but it happened and continues to happen. All matter — all flesh — is literally stuff of the stars. Matter is stardust. Flesh is of the cosmos. There are no real boundaries between matter and the universe, between energy and flesh. All the characteristics of the universe are present in any form of matter. Every grain of sand contains the whole universe. All matter, all flesh, inner-penetrates the entire universe, and the entire universe intends matter to be pleasure and delight. Matter is the place of knowing God, of adoring, and of ecstasy. All the characteristics of the universe are potentially present in the individual. Flesh is a matrix, a seed, which represents all and out of which all can come and grow. It is no longer possible with any degree of honesty to talk about flesh versus spirit, because spirit is matter and matter is spirit. It is no longer honest to talk about body versus soul because soul only manifests itself in flesh, in matter. Matter is a manifestation of soul. The process of transformation — energy into matter; matter into self-organizing; self-organizing matter into self-conscious matter — is the process of energy becoming conscious. Matter is God's process. Priest is matter; priest is flesh; and in flesh transpires the presence of God.

The Talking Lump

The summer between my first and second years of seminary, my classmates and I enrolled in Clinical Pastoral Education (CPE). I became a student chaplain at a state mental institution, a huge facility with a capacity population. Most of the patients were kept docile and controlled by large doses of drugs that rendered them speechless and incapable of controlling some of their physical movements.

As one of my duties, I led a Thursday-morning worship service, reading prayers and delivering a homily for any of the patients on my wing who wished to attend. Several weeks into the program I was conducting a service, and although the usual 20 to 25 patients were there, none seemed to be paying any attention at all. I wasn't sure whether any of them *could* pay attention. I had no idea at all why they were there or why I was really there. There was a large, heavily medicated older gentleman sitting in the front row where he had sat each of the five Thursday mornings before, a rotund, red, sedentary lump of matter and flesh who could only roll his tongue and look at the floor. I became somewhat flip and lackadaisical and started to lead the Lord's Prayer, without having it open in front of me as I usually did (and have ever since). Even if I were to make a mistake, I figured it wouldn't matter very much.

I began, "Our Father, who art in heaven, hallowed be thy name, thy kingdom come, thy will be done on earth as it is in heaven..." And then I drew a total blank. In an instant the man in the front row, who could only groan, roll his tongue, and make guttural sounds, became alert, picked up his head, looked right at me and said in clear English, "Give us this day our daily bread." I carried on from there, and he returned to his former position, his head slumped, tongue rolling, eyes on the floor.

He had been there all along and never missed a word, and when I in my carelessness forgot the words, his flesh (barely missing a beat) was able to burst out of his chemical fog to both teach me and save me.

The Sacred Vortex

It is warm early in March 1990, and while some friends are away, I'm staying for a few days at their hillside home north of Proctorville, Ohio.

Just before midnight I stand on the front porch in the dark, facing south, watching Sirius throb with every color. It utters itself with green, red, blue, and white light. On my right, down in the gully, the creek water resonates, trickling over pebbles and down foot-high falls. Suddenly I realize that the rhythm of the water is the same as the pulsing of the stellar lights of Sirius.

On the left, high above me, is the top of the ridge on the east side of this "holler." The full moon has risen above the ridge but is moving up behind the still leafless trees along the ridge. The moon moves, glowing behind an interplay of branches that lace and unlace in patterns attuned to the tempo of Sirius's pulsing light and the water's sound.

This brings us very near to one another, because despite the different languages of a star, a human being, a creek, some trees, and the moon, we are letting the same wild immensity (and, to us, unsayable plenitude) name and say itself through us. Oh, my.

When the harmless inundation of infinity both from within and from beyond pours into the otherwise empty interior room in each of us, there is a terrible sweet amazement at reunion. Here and everywhere in the creation, the One is somehow awaiting, expectant for the One. So now we know; so now I, too, know the hilarity of reunion with itself of what is everlastingly unsundered.

—Ron Goodman

The Song of Matter

This year I have been driving 50 miles downriver to Portsmouth, Ohio, on Sunday, and then (after a week of teaching at the University) I drive back upriver to rest for the weekend in Huntington, West Virginia. So I have had the honor this year of witnessing spring come to the Ohio River Valley.

Despite the lethal pollution of the air and the dangerous contamination of the water and soil caused by various industries in this area, spring did come again. The trees have awarenesses. And their leaves comprehend that they and the sunbeams are locking into one another's most secret places, thereby healing a great wound in the Absolute — the wound to itself which creation necessitates, when the One becomes Two while remaining One, and the Two becomes The Many while remaining One. And it is, partly because of what they (the leaves and sunbeams) gently are doing that what-is-above and what-is-below, although still separate, are not any longer separated. The wild green chapels where sunlight and tree leaf meet as bride and groom — these woods and weeds — enable a consecrating transitoriness to occur. As consonants and vowels, their joining forms a syllable of praise and sugar.

I hear the sound of a plant. It utters itself. Therefore, in a sense, what I hear is its name. Part of what I know is that the shape of the plant — its root, leaves, stem, flower, and fruit — is another manifestation of its name — its name sounding. But when it sings itself, when it names itself, it does so as a way of offering thanks to the One; and it gives thanks to the One by offering, by sacrificing itself. (The wild mint exemplifies this order of innate generosity. Fragrance is substantive. The wild mint gives itself away, sacrifices itself by releasing its fragrance — like a little sun whose beams are odor.)

And a plant praises. A plant praises by evocation. It calls up out of itself the always-already-there divine imminence. And a plant praises at the same time by invocation. It calls down into itself the divine transcendence.

It is offering itself as a void of space and time, and by this sacrifice, by displacing itself, another "place" begins to exist. A holy vacancy occurs, an inner room for meeting, where the One calls to the One. And then, reunion. That sunbeam and leaf; that syllable.

In several languages the word for spirit and the word for breath and wind is the same. In Hebrew the word is *ruach*. In Lakota the word is *niya*.

Air, wind, breath — these are the vehicles, the "bodies" of spirit. Ancient Hebrew grammarians compared consonants to the body, vowels to the soul. On earth, on this material plane, the soul needs the body to voice itself; and spirit needs the wind, the air, to utter itself, to embody its knowledge and guidance.

To contaminate the wind is therefore a way of silencing spirit, of keeping it from entering this world. True, spirit has other ways of arriving here, but to pollute the air injures this chosen instrumentality. It is an insult to the One. It is in a way an attempt to silence the One.

To keep the holy vowels and consonants apart, to destroy the possibility of achieving the whole and living syllable, can prevent the divine vibration from becoming humanized into speech — into sacred knowledge, into revelation.

The compassion of the One has flowed to all people on earth. Revelation is a portion of this self-sacrificing compassion — spirit sent down to guide the people. To take one example: the giving of the commandments by the One through Moses enabled his followers to know how to live, enabled the humanization of those vowels of spirit to exist.

The commandments represent the wedding of the created consonants with the uncreated vowels; and only thus can an authentic way of life be articulated.

The marriage of matter and spirit fulfills our hope of knowing how to live with and within infinity in our daily finite lives. For in relation to spirit, we humans are the consonants (*con-sonare*, "sing with"). Doing the commandments, we "sing with," join with the holy vowels to incarnate the revelation as those syllables become also deeds. Even the words *pollute* and *contaminate* have a sacred lineage and are synonyms for *desecrate*.

Pollution of the air is a desacralizing of our situation, an amputation of the body (the consonant) from the spirit.

Ultimately, pollution of the air is an attempt to prevent the healing reunion between the imminent *entheos*, the divine within, and the transcendent *theos*, the divine beyond. Contamination of the air is a rejection of that compassion that is implicit in the primal will to incarnation (the sacred syllable) — of the One seeking reunion with the One in the place where the being of human being is a fertile and waiting emptiness — a vigil that could be filled, that could be fulfilled with the covenantal sound of the One's magnanimous and jubilating light.

—Ron Goodman

The Healing Earth

the grass grows longer and longer
the woman walks barefoot through the dandelions
no longer cold
she wonders has the pain stayed with her
through the winter months into spring
the brook runs wild
but the woman holds
her pain close
the cold lets go

but the pain, intense
refuses to move
sadness, anger, loneliness
wrap around her feet
she longs to move
her body
frigid from the cold
she moves closer
to the brook
listening to the sounds
her sounds
her tears
she hears the screaming inside her
body
sadness, anger, loneliness
become rage
it moves through her body
first slowly then faster and faster
as the brook runs wildly so does the woman
the screaming moves
to the outside
the screaming continues
as the woman
feels in her body the pain
she turns
and runs through the dandelions
with the power of knowing
she is finally alive

—Catherine Lambert

The Night Walk

We don't find God.
We are found by God.

We don't have a soul.
We are ensouled.

We don't have our sexuality.
We are sexual.

We don't discover nature.
Nature is us.

My associate, Cindy Krum, is an environmental educator, learning and teaching ways of combining the concerns we have for the environment with the concerns we have for psychology and spirituality. She guides individuals and groups on walks *into* nature with the hope that the experiences will be a continual and building dialogue of inner and outer journey. As the mystics say, "What is true above is true below, and what is true outside is true inside."

This winter, in fact, during the first week of the Gulf War, Cindy led, on separate nights, each of my three therapy groups out into the woods by the ocean at sunset for a journey into the transition of light to dark.

We walked in silence. It was very cold, and very dark, and very wonderful.

We came to a clearing, and she asked us to face the ocean and simply be aware, and then to turn and face the forest and trees, and likewise, be aware; and then to repeat that ocean/forest experience three more times. Then, facing the trees, she suggested that we pick out a tree that intrigued us and walk toward it. There was no doubt about which of the dozens of trees called me; as I walked toward it, I saw my life. It was all there. It was not a metaphor or a simile for my life. It was my life.

At this very moment of writing, I can see that tree, and I know exactly where it is; I could guide you there in an instant.

Later as we continued the journey, Cindy asked us to walk into the dark places in the woods. That was not difficult because the woods had become very dark, and there were always places ahead that seemed to be centers of darkness — black holes — and that is where we were invited to walk, into the black holes. Each time we entered a black hole, we were surprised and amazed, because right there in the deepest darkness was light. Perhaps faint, perhaps only the reflection from a frozen puddle, but there was always light in the darkness; the darkness enabled the light.

The darker it became, the more visible the light. Darkness and light were not enemies, and the light was not trying to overcome the darkness, nor the darkness trying to overcome the light; rather, precisely because of the darkness, the light that was in the woods could shine and be bright, and only by entering the darkest places could we find the light.

The war was on our minds, and each of us wondered how we would find guidance and help. What course would we, should we, could we steer? As it became increasingly dark, the stars came out — the beautiful, beautiful, miraculous stars by which we navigate. Again, only by virtue of the darkness were the stars visible, and their brightness increased in direct relationship to the increasing darkness of the night.

I am shaped and formed by the Christian tradition, and I believe with all my being that by entering the darkness and desolation of the tomb — then and only then, there and only there — does God find us and surprise us in resurrection. My counseling practice is based on that belief and has blessed me with so many resurrectional experiences that my belief is rock solid. Yet, here is nature again, not as a metaphor or as a simile but as direct revelation and fact, engaging me in the reality over and over that in the darkness, the deepest darkness there is light, and that the deepest darkness enables the light. Nature is not a metaphor for anything. It is not a metaphor for reality. It is reality — inner and outer.

After the long walk, as each group returned to the group room to warm up and to "process," I was amazed to hear the ways in which the experience had been so immediate and so direct to the other people. The revelations were certainly different from mine, but no less real, or intense, or important.

Psychology and religion are metaphors, and symbols, and signs of the real thing, at least one step removed. Revelation is the real thing. Nature is revelation, and nature is us; nature creates us.

Driving to Canada earlier this year, just south of Houlton, Maine, I saw a large wolf walk slowly across the highway, sit on the side of the road, and watch me. Mine was the only car in either direction. My path had been crossed. Ten days later a hawk flew up from the side of the road directly in front of my windshield, and then off into the sky. Again, my path had been crossed. A week later, my wife and I were walking around an island when we saw a movement in the bushes. A red fox came out slowly, confidently, walked across our path, stopped not ten feet away, sat, looked at us, and meandered on. Clearly, our path had been crossed.

Each one of those three experiences was electrifying, stunning; each had riveted and commanded my attention. I know them to have been visitations. Someone suggested the Trinity, and I found that symbol and metaphor very helpful in understanding, unpacking, and processing the visitations. Yet beyond those understandings are the imaginal memories of those three visitations which remain burned into my consciousness and retain immense evocative power.

The wolf, the hawk, and the fox were what they were. They are what they are — revelation, not metaphor — the real thing.

PRIEST AS HUMANITY

MANY MILLIONS of years ago, something wet and small with fins wriggled out of the slime and ooze covering most of the earth and chose to live its life on solid land. Energy had become matter; matter had become differentiated and self-organizing, and a tiny piece of that self-organizing matter manifested itself as a living earth creature. To this date, the final product of that wriggle from the ooze is the human species — self-organizing matter that has become self-conscious, capable not only of affecting the environment but also of permanently changing the environment and thus altering the evolutionary development of all the other species upon the earth.

Human beings, with our mammalian, reptilian, aquatic, and fleshly heritage, are wet and sexual (sexual in as many ways as there are human beings). We are clever, highly adaptable, vicious as no other species can be vicious, highly intelligent, and yet, while willfully and intentionally self-anesthetizing, also incredibly generous, inspired, creative and lofty, and simultaneously ignorantly self-destructive. All these and all the polarities of the cosmos are contained within the being of every human being. For each of us, because we are human, there is no place to hide from many of the horrors of the cosmos, because they are contained within. Nor is there any place to hide from any of the glory of the cosmos because it likewise is contained within. Hence, as a species, we are terrified of ourselves and of the very fact that we live.

Humanity as a species has evolved several times. We can look back over thousands and millions of years and see clear evolutionary transitions, yet the notion of random evolution somehow does not say it for all of us. If survival of the fittest were the only dynamic of evolution, we humans probably would not have survived. For, in fact, we are not very fit. Physically and structurally there are species much better equipped to survive and inherit the earth than human beings.

So we must look again at evolution; and if we do look more closely, we see that it is more than simply a process of random selection or survival of the fittest. Rather, inexorably, through the mystery of evolution, there was a constant witness and choosing for more and more complexity so that ultimately we have extraordinarily complex human beings with inordinately refined central nervous systems. Behold the miracle of self-conscious consciousness! It would appear that the goal of evolution is ever toward higher degrees of consciousness and thus a focal point of evolution now has become the human species itself.

The next evolutionary leap will not be biological so much as it will be in the structure of consciousness. We are energy having become matter, striving to become self-conscious. At least in this corner of the universe, we are God's eyes and ears. We are each one of us God striving to become increasingly aware. We are the second coming. Each one of us bears the immense burden and glory of serving the process of incarnated energy becoming increasingly conscious. That is our true identity — to be servants of that divine process: our vocation. To whatever degree we cling to any other identity we will be destroyed.

To see priest, therefore, is to see a mean, sordid, wet, sexual, defecating, urinating mammal, a human creature who is at the same time the focus of God's intentionality.

It recalls for each one of us that we, too, are the focus. We are the intentional focal point and the lead person in God's plan to make all things known unto himself and to bring all things unto himself. This priest who recalls for us that we all are priests is one faithful to that process, in whose fleshly body the process is making itself manifest. Priest remembers us as the second coming.

The Reversal

The priest and his wife have each been married previously. The wife's former mother-in-law has been a very important and special person in her life, providing support and nurture, a mother-in-law, but in fact, a mother.

Several years have passed since she divorced the mother-in-law's son and married another priest. The former mother-in-law makes it clear that she wishes to meet the new husband even though the former husband is her son.

The priest and his wife visit her in her home, and even though she has only three weeks to live, she is full of energy and charm and sensitivity. The visit could be a time of intense discomfort and anxiety, but instead it is filled with grace and caring. As they prepare to leave, she mentions that a friend has given her a bottle of holy water from Lourdes, and before they say good-bye she would like the husband of her former daughter-in-law to come as a priest, anoint her with the water, lay hands on her, pray for her healing, and bless her. Using the hands of all those at her bedside and the holy water, he anoints her, prays for her healing, and blesses her.

He is the priest intoning the words of healing for her, yet it is her unordained ordinary woman's re-markable "grace-filled-ness" that effected a moment of remarkable healing for all.

PRIEST AS SEXUALITY

EVERY SEXUAL AROUSAL, whether toward someone of the opposite sex or toward someone of the same sex or masturbatory or whatever, is always at the heart a desire for God.

The experience of God is instinctual. The energy within a human being which fuels and drives the instincts is erotic. The experience of God is, therefore, always filled with the erotic.

Every priest is sexual. Priest is sexual. To be priest is to be sexual. And in living out our sexuality, each of us is unique, energized and full of potential, mysterious, drawing into the Holy Other. Human sexuality is so potent, so mysterious, and so central to the process of transformation, so identical with being human, and so synonymous with being priest that it must not only be a symbolic representation of the nature of God but also, more emphatically, be at the very heart of the nature of God. Talking about sexuality is talking about God. Sexuality is always cosmological and the cosmological is always sexual. Experiencing the mystery and the miracle and the power of our human sexuality is experiencing God.

Human beings come complete. We are a complete unit, capable of being born, growing and functioning in the world.

Yet even though each of us is complete, none of us is the whole or the total; not one of us can represent ourselves as being the totality of the human experience. For there to be the experience of whole humanness, there must be contact with another. Therefore, we are both a statement of, and in actuality living in, a mystery.

The mystery of God and God's ongoing incarnational process are both symbolized by and expressed in human sexuality. If it were not for sexual reproduction between males and females, we would all be clones, identically replicating ourselves one after another, no room for revelation, no space for transformation and newness. So the mystery of completeness — moving and being transformed into wholeness, and wholeness being transformed into the new creation, over and over and over again — is in the reality of sexual reproduction.

Each of us comes to know himself only through contact with another. Each of us is stimulated to move beyond individual completeness toward wholeness as evoked by the other. For each of us, human beings to whom we are drawn sexually are, on the one hand, the same in their humanity and yet, in some mysterious way, utterly alien. It is in their alien otherness that they have the power to evoke Self.

The Highest Urgency

A poet speaks to us, of healing,

> I am not a mechanism, an assembly of various
> sections.

And it is not because the mechanism is working
  wrongly, that I am ill.
I am ill because of wounds to the soul, to the deep
  emotional self
and the wounds to the soul take a long, long time,
  only time can help
and patience, and a certain difficult repentance
long, difficult repentance, realisation of life's mistake, and the freeing oneself
from the endless repetition of the mistake
which mankind at large has chosen to sanctify.*

What is that mistake that "mankind at large chose to sanctify," which wounds us to the soul? The Bible is the story of God's blatant and ferocious and outrageous love affair with his creation, and the mistake mankind has chosen to sanctify is the taking of that book and making it into a dry, oppressive handbook of moral purity, of rules about righteousness and piety. And that wounds us to the soul.

For some reason, we find it almost impossible to bear. We find it impossible to bear and to perceive and to accept the incredibly outrageous gift, the unconditional gift — the grace-filled unconditional gift of redemption. We can't stand that it comes with no prerequisites, no conditions, and no qualifiers. It offends us, threatens us. And so, in order to gain some mastery or control over God, we begin to attach some conditions; we begin to

---

*D. H. Lawrence, "Healing," in *Selected Poems*, p. 114.

have moral prerequisites; we begin to have rules and standards, and it wounds us to the very quick of our souls. The gift of God is unconditional, and the absence or presence of our moral purity is irrelevant, and we can hardly bear that. It is such good news yet so disorienting and so frightening that we choose to sanctify a mistake so that the common man on the street, if you ask him or her what Christianity is about, would tell you that it is about morality and good behavior, not about God's love affair. That's how most of us have it inside of us, too.

For countless hundreds and thousands of people, the Good News then comes to them not as good news but as bad news — oppressive, tyrannical, moralistic — and it wounds them to the soul. When we change our biblical heritage to a moral handbook, we trivialize God, and we insult and degrade the life, passion, and resurrection of Jesus Christ. He did not die to enslave us to another set of rules and moral-purity projects. He died to set us free. *Wounds to the soul.*

In our efforts to save ourselves, in our efforts to maintain some control over grace, thereby putting conditions on the gift, we come up with rules and standards of moral purity, and we inflict them on other people. We take their moral and spiritual inventory. We intrude, and we invade the most sacred places of other people's lives and make horrible judgments about their worthiness or lack of worthiness. We wound people in the name of our righteousness and in the name of

God. We go into people's lives where we have no right to go.

Wounds to the soul. But even more wounding is what we do to ourselves. In our belief, in our insistence that we must somehow save ourselves by making ourselves worthy or pure, we split ourselves; we cleave ourselves right down the middle.

I am a pastoral counselor, and if there is any one thing that people come to see me about it's about the war going on inside: the self-hatred, the self-loathing, the shame, the self-alienation, the fear of themselves because they are split. They have learned to be split — wounded to the core — split between good thoughts and bad thoughts, good feelings and bad feelings, good fantasies and bad fantasies, and good impulses and bad impulses; and they go to war. They go to war with themselves. I have not met a human being yet, including myself, who has not been caught up in this horrible war of self-hatred and self-alienation all provoked and stimulated by the desire to save ourselves by making ourselves morally pure. All stimulated and provoked by the fear of receiving God's gift.

At the deepest point of that split, at the deepest point in the soul of that cleavage, is the split between the spirit and the body, between spirituality and human sexuality.

Every major Christian group in this country is wrestling with the issue of human sexuality, and so we should, because it is the place where we are most wounded — personally, collectively, and as a culture.

In spite of the fact that our scripture proclaims that "the Word became Flesh and dwelt among us"; in spite of the fact that God declared the human body to be the temple wherein he dwells; in spite of the fact that Jesus referred to himself as the aroused bridegroom seeking his beloved; and in spite of the fact that all of the mystics have had to use explicitly sexual metaphors to describe their relationship with God. In spite of all that, we still put our sexuality on the top of morality's ten-most-wanted list. We still see sexuality as suspicious, as offensive, as inherently spiritually impure. It is a horrendous split, a profound wound, to be alienated from one's own body.

What we now know about human sexuality is that at the heart of every sexual arousal is the desire for God...the desire and the longing for God. We also know that the experience of God is arousing; and we know that in our very bodies as God has made us and created us, in our desire and attraction for our beloved, we experience a foretaste of God's desire and attraction and love for us. Our sexual bodies teach us how it is that God loves us. We know that people often speak about the mystery of human sexuality, the mystery that takes us to our very depths, as being the most profound encounter with their spirituality that they have ever had.

Our sexuality is a sacrament and a place of revelation. To be split off, to be alienated, to be hostile in the name of God from your own body and your own sexuality is actually to be cut off from God and alienated from God. *Sexuality without spirituality becomes effete, precious and dead.*

The split profoundly wounds the soul. In the name of trying to save ourselves by making ourselves morally pure so that we can protect ourselves from the unconditional overwhelming generosity of God, we wound ourselves and others in the soul. *Spirituality without sexuality becomes effete, precious and dead.*

Am I advocating sexual license? Certainly not! Am I advocating an abandonment of the Bible? Certainly not! We abandoned the Bible a long time ago when we made it into a moral handbook. I am advocating that we stop wounding other people and ourselves in the name of God.

I am advocating God and God's outrageous gift, a gift beyond comprehension — God's desire to be one with each of us regardless of our worthiness or purity.

I am advocating God's holy book — all of it, not just select passages. The book that tells the story of God's love affair with us.

I am advocating God as incarnation, as choosing to live in and through our bodies. I am advocating God's gift of sexuality as a sacrament and a revelation of God himself — God herself. God help us! God help us to heal from soul wounds and to make right the mistake that has hurt us and hurt others so badly. May we surrender ourselves to the unspeakable gift.

Amen.

Christmas Eve 1976
Portland, Maine

Two hookers juicy and beautiful
in all their tight pants and fake fur
      Glory

in the cold and wet eve
down Congress Street to saunter
ever so purposelessly

Coming upon a young man
of recent post peach fuzz age
standing, stomping, with ringing bell and kettle army
   uniformed

      they stopped

Into some recess dipped a hand
and the kettle was freshly coined
they stayed to linger, to give a few words
to move their bodies a tiny

not enough to frighten
not even enough to embarrass
just enough to warm him from the inside

looked like the incarnation to me ...
      the church pillars said "no"
      but there was no room at the inn, either.

PRIEST AS HERO

HEROES ARE THOSE who go to unknown places for unknown reasons, beyond the borders, over the edge, into new territory because they know they must. There is about priest something noble and brave, something courageous and heroic. Priest is not the cliché hero, nor the stereotype. Priest is not the caricature or the one who makes everything all right, fixing everything, holding the community together. Priest is not the one who upholds local standards or the one who does anything in relation to the community except go beyond. Rather, priests are those who no longer are finding their sense of self from the images, assumptions, or expectations of others but have found the true source of vision and imagination within themselves. They find themselves irresistibly called to be faithful to those internal images of themselves, and thus they have found the community irrelevant as a source of definition and identity. They begin to serve themselves, and go out into the unknown to find and discover what they do not know, because they must.

How attracted, how adoring, and how thrilled we would be if only a "real" hero would appear! We are so starved for heroes that we drape the mantle of the hero over the shoulders of all manner of pseudocandidates — politicians, movie stars, athletes; all wax as temporary heroes, only to wane as soon as their feet of clay are revealed.

Western mythology is replete with images and stories of heroes and heroines of daring word and deed, snatching victory and life from the ominous and present jaws of defeat and death.

We believe that were it were not for these heroes and heroines, our lifestyles — even our very culture — would not have come to be, nor would it endure. We believe that we exist only because of the marvelous deeds of our heroes, and we believe that there is no higher role to which one can aspire. We expect our egos to act heroically in the ordering, controlling, and disciplining of the psyche. We believe that each one of us is at our best when we respond with heroism in the face of the onslaughts of life.

To be heroic is to be strong, invulnerable, invincible, wise, fair, noble, compassionate, caring, and oblivious to one's own pain and suffering. All the characteristics that are opposite of the heroic (weakness, vulnerability, confusion, doubt, impotency, depression, quitting), are looked upon with contempt.

We all know that Jesus in his own time contended with the expectation that he would save the Jewish nation from Roman domination by virtue of military, political, or spiritual heroics. We must admit that in the late twentieth century, we, too, are ripe with very similar expectations of our religious leaders. All too often they claim that indeed they will fulfill those expectations. It is only a matter of time, however, before we are disappointed, because both our expectations and their claims are revealed as fraudulent.

At the same time that we yearn for the appearance of a hero to save us from ourselves, our lives, and our dilemmas, we are a people coming of age. We are a people losing our innocence; we are a people beginning to realize that the deeds and gestures and words of the hero or the heroine are not enough. We are beginning to suspect that the high-minded, noble, righteous, and self-sacrificing use of power is not enough, or is perhaps even the wrong medicine for whatever it is that ails us. What then? Are there to be no more heroes? Has the age of heroes come and gone? Must we drop *hero* from our vocabulary and, likewise, any expectation of heroic leadership from our hearts?

The image of hero that we have been exploring is structured around a central assumption: the hero saves us from moments of powerlessness, danger, threat, confusion, oppression, and abuse by virtue of his or her superior power — military, physical, spiritual, mental, or whatever. The solution to the horrible human power dilemmas and conflicts are solved by the application of that heroic (superior) power. It is this image to which we are drawn. Yet simultaneously, we are beginning to discover that it is corrupt and it fails us.

There is, however, another image, an image that comes to us from the very core of the great religious traditions: the image of the hero as powerless, vulnerable, despised, rejected. Those heroes respond to the horrible dilemmas of human power conflicts not by overcoming them with superior power but by transforming them. By bringing their emptiness, helplessness, and powerlessness to such dilemmas, heroes become agents of transformation. While heroes are not able to prevent or cure suffering, they are willing to bear and embrace it, thereby changing the nature of that suffering.

The *hero with power*, then, is able to reorder and temporarily fix. The *hero of no power* is able to transform. Every solution that the hero-with-power provides simply sets up the next set of issues, dilemmas, and conflicts; the hero of no power changes the whole "gestalt."

Here we have a paradox: The great religious heroes from all traditions have been men and women of immense and ferocious power. However, they have known that power to have come to them only as a gift from beyond themselves. They have known that either to deny that power or to use it in the cause of their own aggrandizement would be a fatal decision. They have, therefore, known no choice but to give over their lives to become agents of that power in service of the One who gives it. Therefore, because the power is a gift, and because they have no choice but to use it in service, they recognize that they are not masters of that power but its servants. These immensely gifted and energized people are the heroes of powerlessness, weakness, and vulnerability.

When we look at priest in his traditional role as parish clergy, we see someone armed with a book, a bottle of water, a cruet of oil, a chalice of wine, and a plate of bits of bread. These, especially the wine as spilt blood and the bread as broken body, are the weapons and tools that he brings with him to every possible human gathering: to celebrations of birth and marriage, to the grief of death and burial, and to all the other major events of our life cycles. Spilt blood, broken body, signs, symbols, and facts of failure, suffering, power-lessness, disease, and death are the only things powerless enough to transform our power-constipated lives.

The Unwanted Gift

The young woman had been coming to him for counseling sessions over a period of many months. Progress was slow but steady, and they had begun to build a trusting relationship.

At this particular session, she came in with her left hand and wrist in a cast, and her fingers very heavily bandaged. She told the following story: A friend's car was stuck in the snow. She had volunteered to help push it out and was standing behind the car, bent over with her hands on the rear bumper trying to lift and push the car forward. The friend found the wrong gear, putting the car in reverse. The car moved back, and the young woman's hand was smashed between the bumper and the tree stump. The damage was severe, the pain almost unbearable. Several bones were broken, and there was the distinct possibility that she might lose the use of two fingers.

During the session she was visibly upset, angry, puzzled, and in a great deal of physical pain. The two of them, counselor and client, tried to work through some of the feelings and begin to deal with some of the consequences; but the counselor could see that she was feeling no relief at all. He tried every verbal therapeutic technique he knew to help her find some relief, but with no success. Finally, toward the end of the session, the young woman, knowing that her therapist was also a priest, looked at him with pleading exasperation and shouted out, "Well, God damn it! You could at least *pray* for my hand!"

This set him back a bit. He had never been very comfortable with laying-on-of-hands and spontaneous prayer and healing. He certainly wasn't comfortable with prayer in a therapy session; but he was also aware that he was out of resources. He had nothing more to offer. He said, "I don't know what else to do." So not giving what he was about to do much credibility, but thinking it might bring her some comfort, he gently took her hands in his to hide his discomfort and stumbled through a somewhat nervous but spontaneous rendition of a request for healing. He felt stupid, awkward, powerless, embarrassed, and helpless. After all, public spontaneous healing prayer was not part of his training to be an Episcopal priest. In fact, this was way beyond the realm of his experience and knowledge, breaking the boundaries of conventional respectability. The session drew to a close. She thanked him, scheduled the next session, and left. Somewhat relieved that the whole thing was over, he went on to the rest of his day's work.

Two days later, there was a phone call from the young woman. Upon returning the call, he heard her say, "I went to my doctor. He can't believe it. We took new x-rays. My hand is completely healed! It's as if there were no broken bones at all, and my fingers will be fine. It's as if there never was an accident. My fingers will be fine!"

He made some semblance of being happy and glad for her, and he genuinely was, but mostly what he heard was his own inner voice saying, "I don't want to know this."

PRIEST AS FOOL

WITH HEART, MIND, AND SOUL, priest pours himself or herself into a passionate proclamation that the celebration of the Eucharist both represents and presents the heart and core of the drama of creation itself. Priest speaks of death, of violent death. Priest holds up bread and wine and says, "This is the body of the Christ." ABSURD. But even more absurd, priest then offers it to us, reminding us that we are commanded imaginally and sacramentally to eat the dismembered limbs and spilt blood. Yet even more absurd, priest intones this is the food and drink of unending life, of heaven, the very act of becoming one with Almighty God. Such a proclamation not only violates our deepest sense of aesthetic taste, our moral values, but also is utterly and absolutely beyond reason and physical possibility; and yet the proclamation is made with a total devotion, sincerity, faithfulness. Either the proclamations of priest are the ravings of a lunatic or they are the absolute truth.

If the witness and proclamation of the priest is of truth, then the world is not what we think it is. Our modes of perception of reality and our definitions of reality are grossly deficient and distorted.

The fool is one who takes the entire world view, the encompassing gestalt, turns it upside down, inside out, shakes it onto the floor so that we might know that what we take for granted, what we think is given reality, is but a mere fraction of the mystery. Priest makes no sense at all, is utter nonsense. Priest feeds us with brokenness and spiltness and death, and we, by cannibalizing brokenness and spiltness and death, are saved.

The Flip

He, in the line at the restaurant salad bar, had put most of his salad together. There were not many croutons left, so instead of using the plastic scoop intended for the croutons, he was using his hand. She, the older woman, standing behind him, commanded in a very loud voice, "Don't do that!" He asked her, "Why?" She replied, "Because your hands are dirty." He, looking at his hands, said, "I just washed them." With increased volume, she said, "I don't care! It's not sanitary!" He paused a bit, looked her in the eye, and said, "Would you rather be sanitary or loved?" She was transfixed. She was shaken to the core. And yet, caught in her own values, she proclaimed, "Sanitary!" He, knowing that the tables had been turned, said "Okay," and took up the plastic utensil.

The Next Step

Looking again and again at that magnificent and heart-rending photograph of the young man standing before the tanks in Tienenman Square, I see Jesus, and I hear him saying: "Man is not made for the Sabbath; the Sabbath is made for man."

This proclamation by Jesus is not to be confined to a narrow religious understanding concerning Judaistic practices; it is, rather, a cosmological statement concerning the relationship of each and every human being to all institutions.

We must remember that the Sabbath was perhaps the most sacred and honored institution among religious Israelites. Therefore, what Jesus proclaimed is that men are not made for institutions; institutions are made for men, for women, and for children. Or, as one of my New Testament professors said, "Jesus came to put an end to religion."

Somewhere in the last 2,000 years, the matriarchy and the patriarchy (both perverted and partial manifestations of the feminine and masculine respectively) embraced in a dance and produced the age of institutions; for a long, long time those institutions provided more life than death. But in the fullness of time (time being one of the inventions of the age of institutions) they have become and are instruments of death. One then came among us to end the religion of institutions, saying, "Man is not made for institutions, institutions are made for man."

Living in the 1990's, we are participants in and witnesses to the phenomenon of institutions becoming increasingly ineffective and corrupt. More often than not, they bring not life but death, death at the hands of the incredible insistence that they continue to exist no matter what the cost to human well-being. Belong, follow, or die. Hence, the history of the human species in the last millennium has been a grievous and unbearable one of endless atrocities. To be sure, there are other accomplishments; but we are known by our ability to inflict massive and grievous institutional injury and damage upon each other.

We must do, then, what Jesus told us to do, namely, identify carefully whatever it is we might expect from institutions. What do we think they can do for us? How do we think they can help us or save us? What do we think would happen for us by belonging? We must realize that by projecting those expectations on institutions, we endow them with magical, larger-than-life quantities and allow them to have incredible power over our lives; in their name we become both victims and perpetrators.

Jesus would have us withdraw those projections from all institutions and find the locus of these powers within. In fact, we must even include whatever we project onto the institution of Jesus; each of us must come to know himself as priest, anointed one, prophet.

If we fail to withdraw our projections and continue to endow institutions with magical pseudo-divine power, they will kill us. They will kill us because they are decaying, and they would rather die and take us with them than allow us to have back that which we have given them in the first place.

As the Buddhists say, "There is a time on the spiritual journey when a person must decide never to belong to anything else ever again."

> I am not made for the Sabbath;
> The Sabbath is made for me.
> You are not made for the Sabbath;
> The Sabbath is made for you.

PRIEST AS
MOTHER AND CHILD

WHEN WE SEE PRIEST, we see those who give of themselves, who stand at the middle, in the tensions of opposites, and who offer themselves — their words, their prayers, their energy, their time, their attention, their vulnerability — and their devotion as nurturers. They nurture their people by feeding them with the body and the blood. The climax of the central act of worship, after the remembering, after the celebration, is feeding and eating. It is an act of giving, an act of nourishment, an act of tenderness and love, as each host is placed gently on the tongue or into the hands and the chalice is carefully guided to the lips.

It is an act of extraordinary intimacy and mutual vulnerability. It is an act of nursing, an act of mothering. Those who receive know that they have been most graciously and gently cared for. They have been fed with food and drink that nourishes that which is deepest within, and they have come to know that God is mother, and they are unto him as children.

There are three things to know — (1) that we are of God, the children of God; (2) that we are called into a closer and closer relationship with God; we are becoming God; and (3) each of us offers our creativity to the world; to be the mother of God. Children of God; becoming God; mother of God.

It is not simply enough to be a faithful, obedient follower, searching out yesterday's rules for godly behavior. We are called to more. The human body is the temple of the Holy Spirit, and by the Holy Spirit we, like Mary, find ourselves impregnated. We find the Christ within, beginning as a small mustard seed and growing and growing and growing. Perhaps our baptism is our insemination; perhaps it is the first quickening to Christ's life within. The pregnancy is long and hard; it is disorienting, frightening, a violation, a disruption of our lives. This thing within, which grows and grows, we know at some point in our lives will demand to be delivered.

It is not enough simply to be a dutiful follower; more is demanded. We are to give forth with some new and unique expression of Christ. The growing pregnancy within impels us to our own creativity, some outpouring of creative insight and act into the world. Because we, like Mary, don't know all there is to know about who the father of this growing Christ within is, we are a bit embarrassed, shy, mortified, perhaps even afraid; we, like all pregnant women, know that to go through childbirth is to face the possibility of death. The child could live; we could die. And we, like Mary, know that on the one hand the child is of us; on the other hand, however, it is entirely new and unpredictable.

To wrestle with vocation is synonymous with being spiritually pregnant. The dynamics are identical, and to give birth is synonymous with attempting to make one's vocation incarnate in the world. The pain, the terror, the blood, the mess, the unknown, the unexpected, and the letting go are the same for a woman giving birth as they are for all of us as we finally go public with who we really are. And just as it was with the Christ Child and all new infants, so it is with our vocations. The infant is exceedingly vulnerable, dependent, and in great danger. Newly born vocations require protection, perhaps even fleeing in the night to Egypt until old enough to stand on their own. Each person has a mother/child relationship and dynamic ongoing within, a struggling with the vocation. Every priest, therefore, is both mother and child within himself. And every priest has a mother and child relationship with the people. Each priest seeks to help them give birth to the Christ within, and to feed and nurture and mother that process while they also seek to help the priest give birth to his or her own priesthood and to feed and nurture and mother that process; thus, the infants can become children and the children can become adults, and the vocations can emerge in all their creativity and glory.

Michelangelo's *Pieta* is precisely just right, mother and child together.

The Christ first came into this world as an infant, and it was not a safe place for children. Every two seconds, a child dies of a preventable disease. Fifty thousand children a year disappear in the United States into the hands of the pornography industry; most of them are never seen again. Children by the countless hundreds suffer physical abuse, sexual abuse, and psychological abuse. It is not coincidental that the higher the per capita spending for defense and armament in a nation, the higher the infant mortality rate. The world is not a safe place for children. It is not a safe place for children on the biological-physical level, nor is it a safe place for children on the psychological-spiritual level.

Each of us has a deep, abiding sense of how dangerous it is to really allow ourselves to become ourselves, to allow the Christ within to be born. We have a sense that there is some huge penalty and price to be paid for that much creativity, for that much vitality, that much magnificence, so we prevent the birthing as long as possible, or when it comes we hide to prevent it. Priest as mother of his or her own child and of all children, in tenderness and kindness and nurturing, seeks to show all of us how to be better mothers for the Christ Child within and for all the children about us.

Christ has died. Christ is risen. Christ will come again — when the world is safe for children. When we have made the world safe for children, the Christ will have been born again. When we have made the world safe for children, the kingdom will have come, and its Lord, a little child, will be running carefree as a puppy dog in the kingdom, for the kingdom is of little children. The kingdom is of little children, the kingdom will come. Priest is one who mothers the world safe for children.

The Nursing

When I became pregnant with my first child, I knew immediately that I also wanted to nurse her when she was born. I had a romantic idea that pregnancy, birth, and nursing were all natural and somehow effortless, grace-filled animal parts of being human. I reveled in the fantasy of my breasts filling, overflowing with nourishment for my child. That there might be something to learn, something I had to do in order to do something so "natural," never for a moment crossed my mind. Images of "our lady, the contented cow," filled my head to the exclusion of all else.

When presented at last with the reality of my baby, and her hard little gums clamped down on my nipples, I quickly lost that romantic ideal. Nursing hurt. My baby's beautiful little rosebud mouth attached itself with ferocity to my breast. She suckled relentlessly, and the milk did just flow. I had to learn how to let it flow, learn how to let down my milk so that it would, in fact, flow bountifully and nourish her. We struggled for six weeks to learn together how to form that most natural of pairings, mother and nursing child. I had to learn to relax, to release the thoughts about the adequacy of my supply. Was this the right side? the right position? Is it too soon to nurse again? too long on this side? All the doubts and questions raised by an invisible action occurring within my body. I could not see or feel the change of my food to milk, blood to milk, and I had to learn to trust that it was happening. My baby and I had to learn to close out the world, and I, my worries and fears. I had to become utterly present to her, the sight, sound, smell, and feel of her. We had to learn each other's touch.

And when I let go and opened myself to the reality of her, to her presence, with a tingle that electrified my body, I could feel my milk let down and start to flow. With the passage of weeks, I became conditioned to her signals, I developed a letdown reflex and no longer had to think about it in order to nurse her. Nursing did indeed become natural. And not only did my body become attentive to the sight, sounds, smell, and feel of my baby, I responded to the mere thought of her with a gush of milk, and the sound of even a strange baby produced the same overflowing abundance.

I thought when I weaned my son three years ago my time as a nursing mother was at an end. Recently I have come to know myself called to priesthood. In my work as a therapist and other places where I have begun to experience myself even now, long before the fact of ordination, to be present as priest, I see the same process at work that I experienced in learning to nurse my children. If I focus my attention on the litany of worries that seem to run through my head much of the time — Am I really adequate to take this task? Will I say the right thing? Am I being too aggressive? Can I really help? What does this person think of me? — then I dry right up. Nothing flows. I feel tight and barren.

As when I nursed my babies, I must let go of all the ego concerns about me and my performance and turn all of my attention to what is happening in the moment right where I am. I must open myself up, allow the miracle to occur without any active assistance on my part, just as surely as I had to accept the miracle of transformation of grain and meat into milk within my body. When I do that, when I make myself truly present, then my "milk" lets down, the milk of healing, love, the Holy Spirit, and it flows abundantly. As I learn to do that, as I repeat that action of letting go, of stepping out of the way, I am aware of the development of a new let-down reflex, of experiencing the triggering of the release of that "milk" in response to the need of strangers, even by the cries of someone for whom I feel very little attraction.

To be a priest, for me, is to be a nursing mother. I must step away from my ego concerns in order to allow the milk to flow, and when I do, it flows abundantly. I must also care for myself as I needed to when I was nursing my babies. I must get adequate rest, and I must nourish myself in order to provide nourishment. I cannot fail to tend to my own needs also or I will have no milk to offer. And I must be willing to be the nursing one as well, to turn for succor to friends, family, and God. Nursing mothers simply cannot function in heroic isolation. And, I suspect, neither can priests.

—Anonymous

The Birthing

"Does your heart suffer?
Do the hearts of those around you suffer?
Then,
you are not yet a mother
you are still giving birth

you are only near to birth."*

---

*Meister Eckhart, *Meditations with Meister Eckhart*, p. 88.

PRIEST AS MASCULINITY

THERE IS ABSOLUTELY no doubt that in this last century the impact of patriarchal energy on the human species has been one atrocity followed by another. Nor can there be any doubt that the patriarchy must be brought to an end.

However, it must be remembered that the patriarchy is a very immature, retarded form of the masculine which is both a derivative of and a reaction to an overdeveloped matriarchy. That men (and sometimes women) must seek their identity in the world by asserting ever-widening circles of dominance over other men, women, children, the poor, the weak, the crippled, even nature itself, is symptomatic of how little men know of their inner selves, how little men are able to find the ground of their being within their own inner experience, and how little esteem and validity men experience in the presence of the matriarchy.

Our culture is afflicted with both the horrors of a vastly underdeveloped masculinity and the illnesses of an overdeveloped matriarchy. Matriarchy and patriarchy are linked in a collusive dance of domination and death.

The effects of the overdeveloped matriarchy are as follows:

- Everything that is important is deemed to have happened in the nuclear family and, in particular, in the relationship between the mother and the child.

- It is thought that the most important inner experiences that human beings can have are emotions.

- The ultimate values in living are considered belonging, membership, safety, and comfort.

When we are too influenced by the matriarchy, the adventure of human life becomes defined by and confined to the mother/child relationship, feelings, and the safety of belonging. In this state we are pleasantly and degradingly domesticated.

It is perhaps safe to say that no human culture has experienced on the collective level the influence of full-blown mature masculinity. So we can only speculate what that might look like. But speculate we must! For the solution to the horrors of the patriarchy is not a return to the already over-influential matriarchy; instead, men (and women) must do the very hard work of discovering the authentic roots of masculinity within their own experience, *not* as a derivative of, or a reaction to, anything external, including other men. Despite the immense popularity currently enjoyed by men's workshops, this hard work unfortunately must most often be solitary. It is particularly here that the Buddhist saying comes to mind, "There is a time on the journey when we must never belong to anything again."

Let us speculate with full-blown healthy masculinity, i.e., "good fathering," that we might come to know that the meaning of our lives was to be found not just in the mother/ child relationship, not just in the nuclear family, but also in the extended family, in the multiple generations of which we are products, in our connection to the whole human species and to the creation, and most especially to the cosmos itself. With good fathering, we would be taught that not only are feelings important, but they are also truth and integrity. We would know that there are things in life worth risking everything for, no matter how bad it feels; the meaning of my life is not confined by the psychological or emotional boundaries of my own ego experience.

Finally, we would come to know that more than in belonging, our destiny has to do with the fact that the cosmos expects something from each of us, and that faithfulness to that expectation will, of necessity, jeopardize all our belongings, even at the same time affording us the deepest ecstatic joy and fulfillment. The meaning of life would shift from safe belonging to faithful — if risky — service. Being a man means knowing how not to die a meaningless death.

Good fathering, maleness, would make the energies of fertility, penetration, insemination, decisiveness, boundaries, and protection overtly available to a people, nay, a species, sorely in need of such manliness.

The Shooting

Like many fifteen-year old boys, he spent his summer hanging around with other young men his age, talking, sharing, having some adventures, being bored.

One afternoon, a group of boys was in the paneled room in the basement of one of the homes in which the father had his gun cabinet. A rifle was taken down, checked to make sure it was not loaded, and passed around from boy to boy. It was about to go back into the gun cabinet when George, who had passed it by the first time, asked to see it. George took the rifle, handled it, and using the telescopic sight, pointed it around the room at several objects, finally bringing the crosshairs to the throat of one of his friends. Knowing the weapon to be empty of bullets, he pulled the trigger. The rifle fired. The bullet destroyed a throat.

Later, when he was sitting in the upstairs front hall of the house, and the ambulance had taken the injured boy away, George began to speak. With him was the father of the household and a policeman. "I hope, I hope, I hope to God he lives! But what will I do if he dies?" The policeman standing over and behind him put his hands on George's shoulders and spoke to him saying, "Then, my boy, you will become a man."

FORTY DAYS

PRIEST AS HOMELESS

WHEN WE LOOK, we see priest, and we see one who as yet has no home. Priest is a wanderer. Priest is a tent-maker; priest is always looking for a home; priest is always going home. Priest is ordained by the church in the great high priesthood of Jesus Christ in the Episcopal Church at St. Alban's, Cape Elizabeth, Maine; but neither St. Alban's nor Cape Elizabeth, neither Maine nor the Episcopal Church, is home for priest. Priest belongs to God, and each of us wanders searching for our heart's desires. Until we find that which we long for, we are not home.

Priest is one who longs for wholeness, longs for completion, longs for God. By that which we long for, you shall know us. We see ourselves in reference to that which we long for. That for which we are longing becomes the primary lighthouse of our journey, and we are drawn toward it. So to know what I long for is to know me. The only way I can define myself is to reference that which I long for, that toward which I am journeying, that which calls me out of myself, beyond myself, toward it; I am never at home, but always longing.

Priest is one who is homeless and whose heart aches

with longing. He has come to love the longing, and love that which he longs for, more than his own life. And the sanctity of human life is experienced again when we meet one who loves that which he longs for, loves that which calls him home more than he loves his own life, his own identity, his own comfort. Only in the anguish of the gap between where one is and where one is being called does one know the meaning of one's life. It is in our homelessness and our longing that we find the integrity of our being. If we had to define our lives within the boundaries of our already acquired knowledge and experience, we would instantly embarrass ourselves with our banalities. If we were ever for one moment safe at home in the existence we made for ourselves, our lives would become instantly void and useless. We are grateful, therefore, in our homelessness, in our anguish, in our longing for, in knowing that we are journeying toward a home beyond us, for we know that our life is also reflected and defined by that beacon.

When we look at priest, we see one who is homeless among all people who have homes, and we are uneasy. For he reminds us who we are and recalls for us that it is in our homelessness that our lives are sanctified.

The Wandering

Ben is nineteen, and his first great love, Carrie, had sex with his best friend, Paul. He said, "Mom, where do you go when your two best friends are gone?" He cried on the phone as we spoke over the distance from Cheyenne to Santa Vera, CA, where he was living. He said, "Hugs help." But I couldn't hug him. He said that the day before, as he sat next to the oven, he thought of putting his head in it to die. Carrie had meant so much to him. So had Paul. How could they?

He had met Carrie his senior year at the Virginia Smoky Mountain School in Smithville. She was bright and playful, earnest, and able to live outside the establishment. She knew how to work, was well read, and had opinions. Her mother was a lesbian, and she said it didn't matter to her. She loved her mother and so did Ben. I cared about her too, spunky Peg, a photographer who had gone to the same college as Ben's father, Duncan.

I am Ben's mother, and I feel so sad and sorry that my son has been so hurt, and that his wonderful love with Carrie has ended so wretchedly.

Ben was not your routine kid. He was very funny, and did magic tricks, following in the footsteps of my brother Dan. In spite of his gift for performing, Ben was reluctant to go public. He was not confident. Neither am I. I have struggled for the small amount of confidence I have, and I wanted Ben to be different. I wanted him to sell himself as a magician and do birthday parties in the neighborhood. He didn't. Ben has been an underachiever. So have I. Ben doesn't seem to see himself as the wonderful, capable man that he is. Coming from generations of alcoholics, is that so strange? We all have been covering up our low self-esteem.

So now he's quit his job and is driving to Silverdust, WY, to live with his pal Sam from VSMS. He's leaving Carrie and his friend Paul, whom he met a few months ago, moved in with and loved, sharing music together and ideas about life. They formed a band and had hopes that soon they'd have enough songs to play for the public. They wrote some of their songs and were happy together until this. Why did Paul have sex with Carrie and betray his best friend? He said they fell in love.

I love my son. He is a gentle man, like my father. My father was so sweet and kind and a drunk. What will happen to Ben? He has already been through treatment for alcoholism but didn't buy it. He uses drugs and enjoys them, saying he's in charge of his life and it's manageable.

Is life manageable? As I sit here hurting because of my son's loss, I am led to reflect on my own journey which has included many betrayals, perpetrated by me and experienced by me. Until now I have felt very little compassion for the people I injured as I blundered through my life trying to fill the huge hole of emptiness. We all learn the adage, "Do unto others as you would have them do unto you." But how many of us have been able to practice it? I will be fifty years old in January, and it's taken me this long to realize that the mothers of the boys I discarded probably hurt a lot for their sons, too, to say nothing of the sons themselves. And what of the wives of the married men I included in my vast search for love? How did they feel?

I am learning about why I did what I did. I used seductions to get a rush, to cover up my real feelings of fear of being bad, unwanted, unacceptable. I medicated myself with seductions but also with compulsive furniture moving, finger picking, over-eating, shopping, and alcoholism. I have been facing those feelings over the last 16 years and am changing. I am still compulsive, but less so. I don't use seductions or alcohol any more. AA and the 12 Steps have helped me to deal with my guilt, remorse, and grief.

Ben's situation, though, has forced me to experience the pain that mothers, sons, and wives must have felt as a result of my recklessness. I am truly sorry for what I did to those people. I cannot condemn Paul and Carrie. I do condemn what they did and what I did. I was wrong, but so needy, so emotionally sick. I am so angry that Paul and Carrie hurt my son.

Ben is hurting right now as he drives along to Silverdust. But he hurts people, too. He hurts us when he refuses to be responsible for his life. He's driving now in an uninsured car. He has accrued $1,000 of driving violations and, instead of paying them off, he bought a motorcycle. If he fails to pay the fines, they will not go away. They will only accumulate interest so he will owe double, triple, or whatever when they finally get him, or they might even jail him. So there he is — our beautiful, sensitive, funny son driving his heart out to Silverdust as I sit here typing my heart out in Cheyenne.

This morning, my pal Freida remarked on the beauty of the changing colors of the leaves at Centerlake as we ran together. And I said, "Yes, and they are dead." She said, "They look like blooms to me." They do. The color is so vivid. The leaves look like flowers in bloom. But they are about to fall to the ground, leaving the trees bare. I expect Ben feels like that now. The leaves of his pain are brightly colored and are falling off, leaving him naked and alone. He will be naked for a while until spring comes. How is it that spring comes?

The mystery of it all. That's what's so amazing about life. We die over and over in our painful moments, but spring comes. We grow new leaves and don't even know how. Even in death there can be exquisite pain and life therein. Our feelings are heightened. We are alive when we get close to death, to losing someone. I think of how it is when we find out someone is terminally ill. That person becomes so much more precious to us. Or I have heard how close men feel to one another in war together. Their lives are on the line, and they care.

Ben thought about killing himself the other day. I have thought about killing myself in the past. One chooses suicide, I think, when he feels hopeless. When we forget that somehow leaves come again in the spring without our causing them.

Life is. We don't make it. If we let it, it happens. You

know the bumper sticker, "Shit happens"; there should be another one saying, "Life happens." Sometimes it's pretty; sometimes it's not. But change seems to be the constant in it all. In AA they say, "This too shall pass." In AA they say to make a decision and turn our will and our life over to the care of God as we understand him. That is what has kept me alive. I'm not running this show. I have turned my will and my life over to a caring, energy-filled God who is bigger than me or Ben or Paul or Carrie and is committed to helping all of us if we ask.

But Ben has no faith in God. His faith is in himself. What does he have in the car with him today as he drives the tired VW Rabbit to Silverdust filled with his hippy clothes, tapes, and instruments? Does he believe in spring? Does he know he'll heal? Does he know he's good, lovable, capable? Does he know he needs to work? Love and work. Freud said they were the two ingredients for a fulfilling life. Does he know that marijuana will kill any motivation he might have to take charge of his life? Carrie's not there anymore to help with jobs or spur him on. Is there something inside him that will? Will he listen to it?

Our daughter Rhonda just called from the university. She said she'd spoken to Ben and Paul and that they both feel awful. Paul knows he's lost his best friend, and he's drinking to soothe himself. Rhonda told Ben that she loves him and will be there for him. Will he believe her? She has scorned him for so many years. He was too weird for her. But she's changed a lot. She wants her family back. She scorned me, too, and it hurt. But she seems accepting now. We have all felt so much pain. The tree of our family was barren for so long. We will all meet this Thursday in Wyoming. Thank God for spring.

—Anonymous

PRIEST AS VULNERABILITY

THE HUMAN BEING DECIDES, usually very early, not to be vulnerable—in effect, a decision not to be human. It would be as if a plant tried to decide not to need water or sunlight and not to have green leaves, as if it were trying to decide not to be a plant.

We begin to develop feelings of shame and guilt; we are afraid of our vulnerabilities, of our own humanity, of our own essence. We end up hating ourselves for being human, feeling guilty about being human. We become our own enemy. We see our humanity as the enemy, as a plant might see its leaves and roots as the enemy.

The human being, when it rejects its own vulnerability, turns against itself, deciding that it can no longer get what it needs — affirmation, love, nourishment — to be human and that its only choice is to become superhuman, to be above vulnerability, to have no faults, to have nothing that is criticizable, i.e., to be *perfect*.

To be perfect in all ways, in some ways, or in a particular way, the human being begins to see himself or herself as superhuman and becomes *addicted* to perfection. Whatever form the perfection takes (respectability, money, whatever), the quest for perfection in that area is seen as a substitute mother. When I can be perfect, then I will be loved; if I'm not perfect, I won't be loved. When I can be perfect, I will be very, very special. If I'm not perfect, I won't be special because I'll simply be a "regular" human being. If I am human — vulnerable — I'll be mocked, seen as a failure, blamed, rejected. But since I am vulnerable because I am human, the part of me that wants to be perfect goes to war with the essence of my own humanity, that is, the plant begins to eat and destroy itself.

The task is to learn how to be vulnerable again. Priest is a guide and model of that lesson we all must learn.

The Blessing

I remember a priest telling the story that during the early years of his ministry in New York City, a crazy man came to services every Sunday. He sat in the balcony above the priest, so that he could spit and drool upon the priest as he conducted the service. After several Sundays, the priest confronted the man, and the behavior stopped. In the confrontation the priest discovered, to his surprise, that it was, of course, nothing personal; it was simply that he was a priest. He also discovered the vulnerability of being priest.

The Absence

"There is a tendency among us Americans, common and obvious enough, recommended by common sense and successful practice, to estimate a person's aptitude for a profession or for a career by listing his strengths.... The tendency is to transfer this method of evaluation to the priesthood, to estimate a man by his gifts and talents, to line up his positive achievements and capacity for more.... I think that transfer is disastrous. There is a different question, one proper to the priesthood as of its very essence, if not uniquely proper to it: Is this man weak enough to be a priest? Is this man deficient enough so that he cannot ward off significant suffering from his life, so that he lives with a certain amount of failure, so that he feels what it is to be an average man? Is there any history of confusion, of self-doubt, of interior anguish? Has he had to deal with fear, come to terms with frustrations, or accept deflated expectations? These are critical questions and they probe for weakness. Why? Because ... it is in this deficiency, in this interior lack, in this weakness that the efficacy of the ministry and priesthood of Christ lies.... What do I mean by weakness? Not the experience of sin; almost its opposite. Weakness is the experience of a peculiar liability to suffering, a profound sense of inability both to do and to protect: an inability, even after great effort, to author, to perform as we should want, to affect what we had determined, to succeed with the completeness that we might have hoped. It is this openness to suffering which issues in the inability to secure our own future, to protect ourselves from any adversity, to live with easy clarity and assurance; or to ward off shame, pain, or even interior anguish.... And this experience, rather than militating against his priesthood, is part of its essential structure. This liability to suffering forms a critically important indication of the call of God....

It is not our weakness that hinders the compassion and the goodness of God. It is often what others count our strengths that now become criteria by which we distance ourselves from others not so gifted, interests through which we discover others as boring or unproductive.... The greatest protection against this terrible pride — masked as religious seriousness or apostolic commitment, as purity about the things of God...is an abiding sense of our own weakness, that searing reminder that as we are strengthened by one who has loved us, so we should support one another."*

---

*Michael J. Buckley, "Because Beset with Weakness" in *To Be A Priest*, 125–30.

PRIEST AS WOUND

THE WORLD is a wound. The world is a gaping wound. As Buddha said, "Behold, the world is monstrous suffering." The struggle for human integrity, dignity, respect, rights, even more profoundly the struggle for human existence, is immensely difficult and often a total failure.

Every individual human being suffers profoundly. The structure of consciousness itself, as we have inherited it, divides us against ourselves, mind versus body, spirit versus matter, conscious versus unconscious, and so the deepest and most profound conflict and alienation exist within the breast of every human. The world is a gaping wound.

Over and over again, consistently and never-endingly, and as it should be, that wound in all its forms presents itself to priest for something. Is it for healing? Is it for relief? Is it for comfort? Where there is woundedness, there is priest. Priest is called to serve each and all, and since each and all is a gaping wound, then priest must serve woundedness.

And how may priest serve? Can priest heal? Can priest relieve? Can priest fix? Can priest remove? Can priest prevent? What can priest do?

There are those who still want to say, "Things aren't that bad." Those voices will expect priest to heal the woundedness, to say, "There, there, it will get better," to respond with some religious wisdom or convenient piety and to offer words that will at least cover up the wound.

Priest must not be seduced by any of those voices, for priest is called to be present within the wound. A priest's place is to be present in the deepest incision, to be present to those who are most helpless, to be present to the shattered, to the broken, to the shameful, and by his presence be witness to and bearer of the truth. Only when the truth of the suffering is fully validated are we open to the grace of God. Priest cannot heal or prevent or relieve or resurrect. God does that, and God does it when we have told the truth about how very bad, how very broken, how very depraved we really are.

The degree to which priest can be present to the woundedness and brokenness of the world is the degree to which he is able to embrace his own woundedness, his own brokenness, his own shame, his own helplessness. Contrary to the expectation of the world that priest be expert master with multiple resources in response to the world's woundedness, priest proclaims to the contrary — that only by virtue of exploring his own woundedness and proclaiming it to its utter depths can he respond to the woundedness of the world itself. Those things that we consider our most hideous liabilities are, in fact, priest proclaims, our most potent gifts. When we see priest, we see one who is wounded and who celebrates his woundedness as the primary resource for healing.

The Bleeding Heart

It has taken me some time to decide whether or not I should write to you. Our next session is not for another three weeks or so, and I have to let you know what is happening.

The hardest part of all is that it is so personal, so far inside, I can only share the events with Barbara as stories or vague feelings. I am writing because you are a priest, and I think that is what I need now most of all.

I suppose the dream I shared with the group a few weeks ago was a kind of unplugging, or a dredging up of some old fears and anxieties. I don't know. Whatever it is, this is what has happened since.

About two weeks ago, as I was driving my car early in the morning, I remembered the dream. It really hit me. I turned off the radio and just gaped. I had dreamed that I was standing on a street corner, brick wall behind me, concrete sidewalk. Above and behind to my right was a painted wood carving of Jesus Christ. His skin was very brown. His robes were red and blue. He held his hands to his chest and in his hands was a beautiful heart — his heart.

I stood there overwhelmed with God's presence. I knew God was to my left; he was fire. As I stood there, people hustled by, bundled up in heavy clothes, hugging their chests. It's hard for me to write what

I felt. I called out to the people. I cried, "Show your wounds! Don't hide them!" As I said this, I saw that I was naked and in the center of my chest was a gaping wound.

I pulled it open with my hands and kept crying out to the people, "Show your wounds." I turned to the image of Christ and held my wound open. I was ecstatic with joy. Christ's heart was glowing and beaming. I turned back to the hustling people and tried to make them understand. We all have wounds, great gaping wounds in our chests. This is where God has touched us, ripped us open with his touch! I saw a great fiery finger come down, and as it touched me, it became a fiery hook and it tore me, tore my chest open, filled me with fire!

The people wouldn't look into my face. They clutched themselves, their wounds, and moved by as quickly as possible. All I could do was revel in these incredible emotions.

When I got home, after remembering all of this, I prayed. For the first time in ages, I prayed hard! I will never forget this. Even now, I can feel the wound in my chest.

This was the beginning of a new understanding of myself, of God. This dream has sent me reeling. I feel as though my life has been turned upside down, inside out. This was totally unexpected.

And finally, what prompted this letter is what happened last night. I was exhausted from work. It was late. Barbara and I were lying on the bed talking about our day. As we lay there, I began to think about Christ. How he must have felt on the cross, the pain. As I thought about this, I began to see Christ on the cross. Soldiers gambling for his clothes. Suddenly, the image changed, and I saw myself at the base of the cross looking up. Christ was there. He bent down from the cross, placed a firm hand on my shoulder and said in a firm voice, "Have I named you yet?"

I snapped awake again with those words. I was astonished, winded, and what did it mean? When I told Barbara, she looked at me and said, "I wonder why this is happening with you so much lately?" And that is where I am now: *Why is this happening?* Why do I want to cry with joy when I least expect it? Why do I want to pray with such conviction? I'm really confused, as this letter surely shows.

I have always thought of myself as an artist, nothing else. I never felt any other calling. But for the first time in my life, I feel like something else. I feel like a priest. It's so hard to say, but when I do say it, I feel like crying again. There are so many things going on and all I can be *sure* of is my feeling of Christ, of God! This is so unfamiliar, and yet, at the same time, so frightening. (Ha! I meant to say comforting.)

I needed to tell someone. I am always waiting to be called crazy or overzealous, but I can't shake the feeling (knowledge) that this is not just me. Something has happened.

I'll end now, or I'll go on and on.

—Ken Bedders

The Confession

Letter from a client to her therapist

Dear _____,

I finished my homework and decided to pass it in early.

PROBLEM: Identify areas of my personality that I feel you don't understand.

SOLUTION: I don't see vast areas where you're in the dark since most of my trouble spots have been discussed in therapy by now. It just feels like you're not aware of the full *depth* of the trouble in these areas. For instance...

A) *Loneliness/The entire "aloneness" of my life* — To feel alone 100% of the time emotionally, even around other people; to not really know what it feels like to NOT be alone.

B) *Distrust of people* — I think you're only beginning to be aware of how firmly entrenched this distrust is.

C) *Vulnerability/Powerlessness* — We really part company here. You're able to stand up for your rights so vehemently that it must be extremely difficult to imagine that protection not being there. In my case, I feel helpless and vulnerable to all situations. Everything hurts, and nothing I do will protect me. That's a source of real fear.

D) *Inferiority/Lack of self-worth* — You have a sense

of your own value, so this is another area where we are miles apart. I have absolutely no awareness of being of any value except by *doing* things. (With no power or value, it's only reasonable to distrust people. They're very threatening.)

E) *Incomprehensibility of emotions (especially positive ones)* — I think you're beginning to understand how totally blank I am when it comes to understanding emotions. It's frightening the little I know about receiving attention or affection. I have to resort to simple concepts like "warm fuzzies" to even explain it to myself.

F) *Sadness* — It's impossible for me to describe how deep and painful the above issues are, so there's no way to really make you aware of all the sadness I feel. It's as big as the universe and never-ending. Even when I'm happy, it's there to overshadow things.

From my perspective, these issues are close to overwhelming and constantly affect my life. Let me give an example: At the end of the last session, you asked if I had been to the fireworks — an innocent question. My answer was no. You asked what I did that evening. I hadn't done anything. In fact, my only Fourth of July celebrating was to go to a cookout at my parents' house which was hardly a celebration. That was a short, closing conversation, and I doubt you had any idea of the pain it caused me. You had struck a raw nerve. I had wanted to go to the fireworks but would never consider wading into a huge crowd after dark by myself. Believe it or not, I could not find a single person on the planet who wanted to go with me (talk about feeling alone). And if I had succeeded in finding someone to go with, my troubles still would not have been over. Being in large crowds like that only allows me to see other people sharing in relationships and being happy at close range. It's not fun for me to feel lost, confused, envious and sad, all at the same time, especially while 50,000 other people around me are having a wonderful time! Being there would have been as devastating as not being there, in the long run.

I hope this has clarified my situation for you somewhat. If it hasn't, don't worry. I don't expect anyone to be very interested, so whenever you understand *anything*, it's quite a surprise to me! See you Wednesday.

—Anonymous

The Sting

In our new St. Louis home we have hung a memento from the tumultuous days of the summer of 1975. It is a photograph, signed by Gerald Ford, in which he is being greeted by me, his rector, at the door to the Seminary Chapel on the campus of the Virginia Seminary in Alexandria. Looking on is Patricia Merchant (Squires), a recent seminary graduate who had joined the parish as a deacon. The picture appeared on the front page of newspapers across the country on that Monday. It covered the entire face of the New York *Daily News.* No one then or now sees in the photograph what I see, which is the secret that needs telling.

While vacationing on Cape Cod, we had watched news reports of the final hours of Watergate, the departure of Richard Nixon, and the inauguration of parishioner Gerald Ford. Friday evening, following the White House ceremony, a phone call announced the new President was considering making his first public appearance on Sunday morning, attending worship in the church where he and Betty had been members for nearly twenty-five years. Back from the beach Saturday noon, we received word that the visit was definite. Later that afternoon, Shirley and the girls took me to Providence to board a plane for Washington and all the excitement leading to the photograph. The days following were heady. For a brief moment, we reveled in the illusion of being center stage in history. It then became obvious all was not well in Eden.

Anna Barton (Thomas) had been on the church staff for two years as Lay Minister, an innovative and demanding kind of ministry we shared in creating. A few days later, her anger and frustration erupted. In the midst of the excitement, she sat on the sidelines as an observer, especially observing what the photograph revealed of two of the three "ministers," one of whom had been part of the team for less than three months. Anna was not to be seen. She spoke of the hurt and how, if I really believed in lay ministry (and, in particular, the kind of lay minister *she* was), I had missed an opportunity to say so to the world.

I simply explained to her about what clergy do after worship on Sunday. It would not occur to me to include others. It is always the rector and ordained ministers who greet the congregation at the door and not the organist or sexton or senior warden or parish secretary. She should not take it personally. That is how things are.

Anna said to me, "It's that way because it's the way you want it. All you had to do was walk over to the Secret Service man and tell him you wanted me to stand beside you, and I would have been there. You had the power to change what always is, and you made a decision to keep it the same."

The truth stung. The church and every other institution, tradition, and relationship stays the way it always is because the people with power choose not to change it; for reasons known and unknown they prefer to keep things the way they are.

Mark and Matthew tell about Jesus the Jew intent upon being faithful to a calling to seek only the lost sheep of the House of Israel. To help the unknown Greek Syrophoenician woman begging for her daughter would be like casting children's bread before a dog. Yet, because she was so stubborn or desperate enough, the woman persisted in importuning Jesus three times. When he assured her the little girl was healed, there is the implicit sense that something within him had shifted. Her faith that Jesus describes as great is evident in her unwillingness to let him stay where he is. She challenged what he had believed to be God's destiny for him, (not just his preference). Jesus discovered in his struggle with the nameless woman that he was wrong; his idea of mission was too narrow, his image of God too exclusive. In the process something has to be let go and be sacrificed, broken for the sake of an even higher value.

Being a priest means bearing apostolic authority within the holy catholic church. When hands are laid upon the head, one is, indeed, symbolically empowered in mysterious ways both inwardly and outwardly. It means responsibility for numerous things such as blessing and consecrating and absolving. The power is about the stewardship of gifts of God for the people of God. It is a lofty, humbling, and very dangerous place to be.

As priest, the ordained one is recipient of untold projections of a longing deep within the human soul for another able to save, heal, convince, inspire, cleanse, and make new. The archetypal messianic yearning characteristic of being human is familiar to us in Hebrew scripture. It will soon be focused upon every too easily inflated mortal kneeling before a bishop. The newly ordained quickly experience it. The tone of voice, the look in the eye, and the abiding deference to collar quickly spin an invisible web.

With the power come the expectations of the flock. One who can turn wine into blood and who can loose the bonds of sin in heaven and on earth logically becomes spokesperson for God in all matters doctrinal, parochial, and social. It is a propensity that comes to be expected, accepted, and even encouraged. The unconscious priest most often attributes parishioners' demands to a vocational burden needing to be carried. Ultimately such hubris produces a religious icon who, like a magnet, draws such projections. If one is lucky, the inflation eventually leads to a breaking, allowing the possibility of new birth, though there are no guarantees of the birth of a new person. Should the priest be one of the few chosen among the many called, the path will lead to shedding of blood, death, and a resurrection.

As priests we hold on to "how it is" despite the pain and carnage (even with all the woes and the wailing) simply because somewhere deep inside we choose to keep it that way. We are the ones with power to make it different. We usually do not. It is the priest who ultimately must let go of word, sacrament, and ministry if others are to break through old patterns and take a religious journey with promise. When it does happen, a price is paid on both sides of the altar rail.

At the church door or at a table, in a discussion group or vestry meeting or in an office, the priest is deciding, always choosing to keep the world the way it is or serve the holy process of transformation. Every human being is likewise making the same choice. The uniqueness of the priest is a mantle of numinous power requiring finally to be sacrificed. Jung contends there is, indeed, no movement toward individualization and wholeness, no resurrection and new life, without dying. The ego, so fragile in most of us and so greedy for whatever will empower, ultimately must suffer a defeat and be wounded if one is to encounter the *self* that Jung describes as the *imago Dei* within us. The Holy Other waits for the breaking of the egocentricism of the holy vessel, when the yearning part of us seeking wholeness discovers that what is needed is not to hold on but to let go.

"It's that way because it's the way you want it," Anna said to me. In most of life, whether we know it or not, we get precisely what we want. Healing of the priest is on the other side of consciousness, requires wounding, and leads through a cross. Such healing is possible only at great risk. Its stakes are as high as life itself, for not only the priest but for every man, woman, and child who is greeted each Sunday at the church door.

—The Rev. William Dols

The Drowning

Over two years ago, she made her first appointment as a client, suffering deep, deep depression that sometimes brought thoughts of suicide. The woman is thirty-five years old, divorced, a single mother.

Six months ago, she came in for her regular session. "I want to ask you about baptism," she said. I was surprised, because even though she knew that I was a psychotherapist and an Episcopal priest, the subject of religion had never come up.

I responded to her quite simply, telling her that baptism is a ritual of drowning, going down beneath the surface, dying, being transformed, and rising up into new life. We talked a good deal more.

Then, three months ago, she began her session by announcing, "I have decided that I want to be baptized, I want my two-year-old daughter to be baptized, I want my fourteen-year-old son baptized, and I want you to perform the ceremony."

The baptism took place on a beach, at a breakwater, on the coast of Maine, with a small group of friends and loved ones. Saltwater from the ocean was used as the water for baptism. It was a stunningly beautiful day.

What made this baptism so profoundly remarkable — and yes, baptismal — was that the baptism was taking place at the same spot at which her younger son had drowned two years earlier. He and his older brother had been caught on the breakwater in a storm as the tide came in, and he had died in his brother's arms as the boys awaited rescue.

So the place was, indeed, a place of drowning, and the baptismal water was also the water of death. And the son who went into the ocean to fetch the baptismal water was the same son in whose arms the little boy had drowned. The daughter was being carried in the womb of her mother at the time of the drowning.

But on this day, out of the drowning, out of the water of death, came a rising up, a transformation. Baptism: the ritual of drowning and new life.

PRIEST AS SILENCE

WHENEVER AT A GATHERING a human being wearing a white plastic collar enters and is recognized, a shock wave of emotion and significance shudders through the entire gathering. It matters not whether the priest is a stranger or well known, whether the priest is liked or disliked, or whether the priest has uttered a single word. The presence of priest — even as silent and unknown — releases a tidal wave of energy. It is not what priest says or does; in fact, the priest need not to do or say a thing. It is simply that priest *is*, and then the tidal wave rolls on.

A baby at some point begins to search the eyes of its mother and of other human beings for recognition, for validation, for affirmation, for identity. That process of seeking identity in the eyes, in the behavior, in the gestures and actions of others, continues through childhood, adolescence, young adulthood and throughout our entire life. Our personalities, our social interactions, our accents, our figures of speech, our thought processes, styles of walking, all are shaped and conditioned to the people and groups with which we most closely associate. We live our lives consciously and unconsciously seeking to fulfill the expectations and the agendas of other people and groups. We thus constantly seek permission and validation in our expression of the emotional life, the intellectual life, the spiritual life, and in the creative life. We learn that our lives don't belong solely to ourselves, and that in fact, our okay-ness, our worth, our validation, are in the possession of others. The world then overflows with a cacophony of sights, sounds, gestures, approvals and disapprovals of others. Even when we are quiet, there is no silence.

This becomes an intolerable way to live, and the realization gradually dawns that perhaps a person might withdraw the search for identity and validation from those around him and instead begin to look within. A person could discover a powerful and sacred agenda for himself deep inside, one more powerful and more sacred than he had ever heard or seen coming from others. A human being could enter his own aloneness and discover how to be faithful to his own soul, never again to be subject to the self-betrayal and the seductivity of trying to shape his life by the affirmation and approval of others.

This is the beginning of a journey of solitude. In renouncing the siren calls of the world, entering into one's aloneness, one discovers the deep self, resonating within, a self-validating authenticity, a center of truth — a center with which one in solitude can connect and may never be willfully disconnected. This connection is maintained and strengthened, deepened and bonded, in silence. Priest is one who has found this center, is called to it, and is ardently grateful. Priest is one who knows that all the voices of the world are voiceless and illusory, and that only in silence and in solitude can one hear the true voice, the voice from another order. Priest knows that freedom and faithfulness, joy and love, come not from the hollowness of the voices from the world, but from the wholeness of the silence within.

So in the midst of social gatherings full of empty noise, priest enters in fulfilling silence, and the tidal wave is set free again. In the presence of those bound in the servitude of pleasing others, priest is liberated for true service.

Henri Nouwen says it this way: "Solitude is the furnace of transformation. Without solitude, we remain victims of our society and continue to be entangled in the illusions of the false self. Jesus, himself, entered into this furnace. There, he was tempted with the three compulsions of the world: to be relevant (turn stones into loaves), to be spectacular (throw yourself down), and to be powerful (I will give you all these kingdoms). There he affirmed God as the only source of his identity. (You must worship the Lord your God and serve him alone.) Solitude is the place of the great struggle and the great encounter — the struggle against the compulsion of the false self, and the encounter with the loving God who offers himself as the substance of the new life.

We have to fashion our own desert where we can withdraw everyday, shake off our compulsions, and dwell in the gentle healing presence."*

---

*Henri J. Nouwen, *The Way of the Heart*, 13.

The Anonymous Accomplice

I write this without being yet a priest, because I have known it to some degree merely by kneeling by the altar as server. The broken Host lies on the paten. But the fact that you are in possession of the secret, identifies you with the Saviour and with what is going on. And without words or explicit acts of thought you make assent to this within yourself simply by staying where you are and looking on.

There Christ develops your life into Himself like a photograph.

Then a continual Mass, a deep and urgent sense of identification with an act of incomprehensible scope and magnitude that somehow has its focus in the center of your own soul, pursues you wherever you go; and in all situations of your daily life it makes upon you secret and insistent demands for agreement and consent.

This truth is so tremendous that it is somehow neutral. It cannot be expressed. It is entirely personal. And you have no special desire to tell anybody about it. It is nobody else's business.

Not even distracting duties and work will be able to interfere with it altogether. You keep finding this anonymous Accomplice burning within you like a deep and peaceful fire.

Perhaps you will not be able completely to identify this presence and this continuous action going on within you unless it happens to be taking place formally on the altar before you: but at least then, obscurely, you will recognize in the breaking of the Bread the Stranger Who was your companion yesterday and the day before. And like the disciples of Emmaus, you will realize how fitting it was that your heart should burn within you when the incidents of your day's work spoke to you of the Christ Who lived and worked and offered His sacrifice within you all the time.

—Thomas Merton*

New Seeds of Contemplation, 162–63.

PRIEST AS SINNER

CONVENTIONAL MORALITY is, at best, a reflection of the given culture's operational assumptions, norms, and values. What is best for the collective is that the collective continue in as stable a modality as possible. Morality then becomes a reflection of the collective's primary valuation of self-maintenance and stability.

To discover the heart of a particular morality requires discovery of the fundamental organizing dynamic of a particular culture.

Ken Wilbur, in his book *Up from Eden*, has said that the fundamental organizing dynamic of our culture has been and is the "dilution of vitality." He further states that the primary product of Western culture is the dilution of vitality for the purpose of diminishing consciousness and awareness to its lowest possible point so that the collective and individuals within the collective do not have to be aware of death and their own mortality. The more vitality is diluted, the more illusions of immortality can flourish.

The morality of our culture, therefore, should and, in fact, does reflect that basic organizing principle.

What the morality then deems as good are behaviors, institutions, forms, emotional sets, expectations, relationships, personalities, whatever serves the cause of diluting vitality. Feeling states such as hopelessness, despair, depression, inadequacy, stupidity, abandonment, rejection, and behaviors such as failure, illness, and impotency, are very subtly, but very clearly, approved of and deemed good. On the other hand, such feeling states as passion, excitement, enthusiasm, intensity, arousal, delight, playfulness, and behaviors such as competency, excellence, creativity, self-investigation and awareness, love, faithfulness, commitment and tenacity (while they may feel emotionally good and terrific), are deemed by the culture as bad and unacceptable. Such feelings and behaviors generally produce disapproval, envy, and discounting. Persons exhibiting those behaviors are often isolated and excluded.

When we see priest, we see one who has enthusiasm (in-God-ness). We see one who witnesses to and proclaims abundant life, calling us to the table of mystery to celebrate the heavenly banquet of overflowing and overwhelming grace. When we see priest, we see one who sings and dances with exuberant joy in the sure and certain knowledge of the resurrection of all things. When we see priest, we see celebrant. Of all people, priest is called to be one who is immoral and calls all the rest of us to become immoral, too. The royal priesthood of God stands in utter opposition to the notion of our present culture that the good life is the safe life, the diluted life, the respectable and responsible and grown-up life of diminished vitality.

God is vitality, and God is in us, and we are in God. And we sing as priests with all our beings that the precious gift of vitality is not to be diluted, but to be cherished, enhanced, and gloriously lived out in our own bodies, in our words, in our eyes, in our hands, and in our lives. In the eyes of our own culture, we are called to become profoundly immoral, the sooner the better.

The Wish

Things go by.
I see the litter of petals
below the peonies.
Even the lavender cloud-heaps,
which seem so heavy edged in gold,
will dissolve.
Swallows dip to the pond
in twilight, wetting their wings,
nipping the life of newly hatched bugs.

I look up at her open window,
the curtains hanging still,
unmoved by the trills of frogs.
I think of her sleeping summer sleep,
her eyelids lavender,
her golden skin brimming in repose.
How will I live
when her rambling farms
of wooden blocks
no longer cross the floor?

She will not always bring me
fireflies;
I will not always smooth the sadness
from her petal face.
I know Death is there
when I kiss her good-night.

"If I were an animal that stings,"
she said,
"I wouldn't."
Learn to sting.
Embrace your nature.
Make your link with the holy chain.
Then, only then, will I know
That God won't let you end.

—Anne C. R. Leslie

PRIEST AS
COURAGEOUS COWARD

IT IS EASY (in fact, some people make it a lifetime occupation) to rebel against perfectionistic societal and cultural expectations and norms. It is far more difficult to become faithful to the compelling internal images rising from within the deep *self*, images of excellence and fullness of the *who* one might become.

To evaluate oneself constantly against the stereotypic perfectionistic norms of society nourishes an internal crop of anger, resentment, depression, and sullen compliance of testy hostility. On the other hand, to hold oneself accountable to the images of the divine within is painful and fearsome and wonderfully healing and humbling. The perfectionistic expectations of the culture, while tempting in their promise of status and righteousness, prove to be barbarically inhumane and deceivingly shallow. The intimations of glory from the callings within are more than tempting. They are overwhelming and inundating; they prove to be the very essence of life.

Each one of us has the God-given and grace-filled invitation and opportunity to grow and be transformed into the fullness of our own Jesus-likeness. In responding to that invitation, there is a time (which may last for years) when we first become aware of the images arising from the internal *self* that we might become, and yet find ourselves still living the old life. The contrast of the new awareness and the old life, the contrast of the inner reality and the outer reality, creates a gaping and profoundly unsettling disparity. This is a time of struggle and torture. Living in that space between who we are and who we know we might be and are called to become, living that gap between our images of God and who God really is, is exciting and devastating.

The gap between awareness of future potential and actual realized potential is on the one hand our maker's responsibility, for that is how we are made. Yet, on the other hand, somewhere within we know that we have willfully and morally contributed to the creation of the gap, or at least to prolonging its existence. We want to become who we are called to become. We want to close the gap, and yet we do not want to become who we are called to become.

We do not close the gap. We hesitate. We resist. We put off. We deny. We sweep under the rug. We forget. We become preoccupied with all manner of other things, for to close the gap is to be utterly transformed, and that is death: fright unto terror, the terror of inundation. It is the terror of surrender, the terror of transformation, the terror of baptism and eucharist, drowning and crucifixion.

We know it is partially by virtue of our own cowardice that our gap continues. Learning to live with ourselves and

accept ourselves and love ourselves as cowards is humiliating. Instead, many of us choose to return to the combat
of conforming with or rebelling against societal expectations rather than maintaining ourselves in the holy gap.
The gap is excruciating for all its possibilities of wonder
and joy and for all of its humility and humiliation. For
a person to stay conscious of and faithful to the internal
images of *self*, and thus stay on the journey toward what
God has in mind, is at the same time to have to live with
and embrace oneself as a profound coward. Paradoxically,
the moment we embrace ourselves as cowards, we find ourselves standing waist deep in the courage it has taken us to
make the embrace.

Over the years, step by step, grace by grace, by crucifixion and resurrection, the gap begins to close, and one's
sense of oneself as coward begins to diminish, but there is
no avoiding this stage of the journey.

Of all the struggles in a priest's life, it seems it is this
struggle that is, on the one hand, perhaps the most jeopar-
dizing thing priests can do, i.e., to reveal themselves to those
whom they serve. On the other hand, it is the most precious
gift they have to offer those whom they serve — sharing
openly, honestly, and joyfully with those around them. Without priests who are willing to share this struggle openly
and honestly, willing to be courageous cowards in a public
way, the worshipping community will regress into believing that it is conformity with the external norms of culture
and society that is at the heart of religion; the worshipping
community will then be lost. The presence of verbal witness
by courageous cowards to the reality and unique value of

their struggle calls the worshipping community back out of perfectionism into the deepest reality of glorification. This is priest's greatest risk and greatest gift.

The Betrayal

Dear, dear Judas:

I miss you. I miss you very much. So many hopes, so many excitements, so many fears we shared, you and I. We all miss you.

When you left at the supper to betray him, I was relieved; I knew that I would not be the betrayer. But the relief and the smugness didn't last long, for just that night, only a few hours later, we couldn't even keep watch with him; we fell asleep, and later some of us were identified as his companions, and we denied ever knowing him. The next day, we let him die, and some of us didn't even dare to be present while he suffered; now we are all hiding in our holes in the ground like rabbits.

Judas, Judas, oh dear Judas, your suicide is so tragic. Don't you know we all betrayed him, all of us, every single one of us more than once, several times? I realize now that while he was alive before the end, we betrayed him all the time.

Judas, Judas, to be with him, to follow him, to love him, is also to betray him.

Your arrogance, Judas, your damn arrogance and pride. Who in God's name were you to think that you were more than us, or was it that you thought you were the first? You didn't have to die, Judas.

Each of us has had to live with the same self-knowledge that killed you. To betray him is humiliating and shameful, but we can bear it and so you could have, too.

And what's more, and more blessed, and also more humiliating — his love for us grows. He appears in our lives; in our shame, and utter unworthiness, he embraces us. There is no hiding from him, not even in spitting in his teeth. Betray him, reject and hate yourself, wither in shame — there is no escape, no hiding. You cannot make him let go.

I suspect, Judas, even where you are now, that he won't let go. Judas, Judas, my brother Judas, do you hear me?

We all betrayed him and will betray him again. You didn't have to die. He won't let go.

Judas, I loved you, and I miss you.

—One of the Twelve

IN THE TEMPLE

PRIEST AS SERVANT
OF CEREMONY

THERE ARE THOSE who say that our dreams are about our lives, but there are others who know the opposite to be true — that our lives are about our dreams. It is images (verbal images like poetry, metaphor, musical images, and most particularly visual images) that impact and shape the deepest recesses of our being. The dream is a visitation to the individual. Ritual and ceremony are a visitation to the community. Ritual is to the congregation as the dream is to each member.

Ritual and ceremony should tear our hearts out. In the experience of authentic ceremony, the community is changed, transformed. Normal time and space are suspended, and the congregation moves into an experience beyond reason, into drama and image. In ceremony, all five senses are stimulated with music, with color, with movement, with smell, with light, with touch. In ritual, the whole congregation becomes involved in the restatement, reenacting, and remembering of the great themes of human and divine interaction. The involvement can be so deep that the whole people gathered becomes the incarnate image of the proclamation. When this happens, not only can we say our lives are about our dreams, but corporately we can say our life together is a reflection of and response to our ritual. The shape of the liturgy, the rhythm and flow of the ritual, the image of life that the gathered folk achieve in ceremony, becomes the most formative impulse in the shaping of our life from birth to death, and even after death.

At the center of the magnificent, miraculous, and awesome transformational process stands the priest. The priest is not the ceremony. The priest is not the master of the ceremony. God is. The priest is not the host of the ceremony. The Lord Jesus is. The priest is the servant of this miracle called ceremony, and it is the priest's job to assure that the ceremony is accomplished with as much imagination, and as much depth of drama, as much involvement as possible of the five physical senses of the people there. There is no more important function a human being can perform.

The Embrace

It was her fourth birthday party. She and her friends had just bought ice cream from the traveling ice cream man, but as she walked out from behind the white ice cream truck, she walked right under the rear wheels of an oncoming fully-loaded coal truck. If someone hadn't yelled, he wouldn't have known to stop. There was nothing that could be done because there was very little left of her at all. The children, the little girl's mother, some other adults, and the truck driver — a large overweight middle-aged man in a coal-stained sweaty T-shirt — stood mutely in a circle. There were one or two attempts at pious utterings: "God takes the little ones first because he loves them most;" "She's better off now that she is with God." The silence was piercing.

The little girl's mother, a small woman, began to weep and scream and beat on her head and face with her fists. As she stood there and beat on herself, everyone else stood in frozen paralysis. We stood there for a long time.

Then without uttering a word the truck driver opened his arms, turned his hands outward, and looked at the woman. She walked slowly toward him into his embrace. He wept. She wept. The freeze was broken. The silence, the paralysis, was broken. We all wept. We wept. We held hands. We hugged.

The little girl was dead. We were dead, and with the simple motion of lifting up his hands and arms, the truck driver had offered us a ritual that gave us life and transformed us.

The Birthday Party

Each year, in November, I am invited to facilitate an intense weekend workshop in St. Andrews, in Canada, entitled Spirituality: Authenticity and Vocation.

It was Saturday evening of this year's workshop, and the participants had become very close, very open, very vulnerable.

A man had just picked up his talking stick to do his piece of work, when there was a knock at the door. We knew this to be most unusual, because we were in a cabin far off the main road, in a little coastal village almost empty of people.

The man with the talking stick opened the door, and standing there was a Royal Canadian Mounted Policeman (we had been talking about God coming among us as a stranger). In an instant, we all knew that the only reason he would be there was to deliver bad news. Which one of the twelve of us would it be for?

He quietly spoke a woman's name, and the woman came forward. She accompanied him outside, returning a brief time later. She said that she was "okay," then burst into tears.

The twenty-year-old son of a close friend had been killed in an automobile accident. In our openness and our vulnerability, we were all stunned, struck, in shock.

The woman stayed with us — and we with her — as she made the necessary phone calls, weeping continually. It was a descent into hell. It would be some time until her husband arrived, and we spent that time grieving with her. She told us that she had never been so blessed, so prepared to deal with the people back home that she loved so much. Someone had brought incense, which we burned to cleanse and purify.

Finally, there was no more to do or say. Coincidentally, it was the birthday of another woman participant, and members of the workshop had earlier that day bought a cake, some candles, ice cream, and a few small gifts. There was nothing to do but celebrate.

What a wonderful birthday party we had! We made wishes on the candles and played with the crazy foam. The woman whose birthday it was cut a slice of the cake, took a small piece, then fed the person next to her. And thus it went, from person to person, feeding and being fed.

The grieving woman's husband arrived, and she left us, sad but fed and uplifted. We had not celebrated a ritual–the ritual had celebrated us.

PRIEST AS JUDGE
AND ABSOLVER

THE ARCHETYPAL ENERGY of priest is witness to, symbol and proclaimer of, the great unconditional oceanic love of God for all and each — the love spoken over the head and into the ears of his Son and at the baptism ("Thou art my well-beloved Son in whom I am well pleased"). It is a love that enfolds each of us as if in the soft and caressing wings of a dove, a love that loves us to the core.

Because we are loved to the core, we are pierced to the core. We are known to the core and all and everything about us is made known to us and revealed to us. Most paradoxically in the very moment we are most deeply loved, we become most deeply aware of our depravity; the very moment that we are most deeply embraced, we become most deeply aware of how totally unworthy we are of the embrace. We are drawn to priest for the love, and we are repulsed and terrified by the judgment dynamic of the love. We come to see the utter completeness of our sinfulness: the sins of violence and brutality against others and ourselves; the sins of inflation and superiority and grandiosity; the sins of false humility and false inferiority and deflation; the sins of pride and greed; the sins of self righteousness; the sins of pleasure in other people's failure and pain; the sins of knowing that we would rather lie to ourselves than face ourselves, that we would rather sacrifice other people than face ourselves; the sins of knowing that we are aware of who we are called to be and refuse to become because it is too risky — all the sins of reinforcing and justifying and protecting the illusions of our puny little egos. We sell out so much for so little.

Then we know perhaps the worst sins of all, the sins that blaspheme the Holy Spirit, the one who brings power and options and possibilities, the one who speaks directly to our imaginations and asks us to know more, see more, vision more, hope more. Blasphemy is sin against the imagination: concretizing, fundamentalizing, literalizing, cynicism: these kill the spirit.

So in the presence of priest we are revealed to be utterly corrupt and depraved. There is no place within that is without contamination. There is no imaginable way with which we can justify our existence.

The wonder of it all is, of course, that until we can acknowledge our utter depravity, we are not free. For as long as we are attempting to manufacture or put forth a self-image that will somehow stand up under the scrutiny of judgment, we are not free, we are slaves. Only by acknowledging and embracing our utter depravity can we remove ourselves from the useless rat race of self-justification, and only in the presence of God's total love and desire do we dare do that.

If for a moment we can catch a glimpse of what it's like

not to have to worry about justifying ourselves, then we will catch a vision of how everything is a miracle, how everything floats in and upon a vast ocean of tender grace. The miracle is that we exist at all. It's not that our lives are a little bit tarnished and that God occasionally sends a pinch of corrective grace. It's that our lives have no justification at all and, in spite of that, are totally shot through and through with grace. It is an ongoing, incredible miracle. In the excruciating humiliation, pain, and presence of that ego-destroying judgment, we can then come to desire God as much as He desires us. All this is in the presence of priest.

The Celebration

Letter from a Young Woman to Her Father

Dad,

I have thought a great deal about a meeting between us since I last spoke with you. As a result, two important realizations have occurred to me.

The first involves timing. I realized that when I talked with you on the phone, I failed to state my purpose for wanting to have a meeting. Specifically, the topic I most want to discuss with you is the time period between when I was approximately eight, to age thirteen when you sexually molested me. It has taken me a long time to clarify my reasons for wanting to discuss these events with you. After much thought, I feel the most important reason is to end this burdensome secret of incest. It is necessary for me to now shed this burden. I feel that the secret will be completely discarded only when we are able to discuss these events openly. Within the last two years, I have been able to openly discuss with the other members of the family the fact that you sexually molested me, but not with the most important one — you. I don't want to "get" anything out of this meeting. I don't want money, I don't want revenge. All I want is freedom from the burden of the secret.

The second also involves timing. I have been in therapy on and off for three years. However, as I understand it, you have been in therapy only a short time. It is most likely that your timing, in terms of being ready and willing to take part in a constructive meeting between us, is not on the same schedule as mine. In my enthusiasm to proceed forward in my therapy, I wanted to rush right into a meeting. However, I failed to take into consideration your readiness. It is important that we both be emotionally and psychologically ready to take part in a meeting. I don't want to pressure you, or challenge you, or scare you, or any of those terrible things my abrupt announcement might have done. I want us to go into this meeting on equal footing, without hostility, or defensiveness. I want us to simply be able to talk.

Please feel free to take your time in thinking about this. It is not important to me when this meeting takes place, but it is important to me that it does take place at some time. Please share this letter with your therapist and talk to him about it. When you feel ready, have him contact my present therapist, as I do not wish to be contacted directly by you at this time. Then, perhaps, they can decide if we are indeed both ready.

I have sent copies of this letter to Mom, _____, _____, _____, and _____ as well as _____, because I feel it is another important step in ending the secret. I have felt free to discuss the incestuous incidents with them in the past, and I want you to feel free to also discuss these with them if you so choose. I feel it is time we stop saying there is nothing wrong in this family.

I have a problem. I want to talk about it. But I need your help and everyone else's help to do this. Let this be a celebration, an end to the deep dark secret that has affected our lives in such negative ways. Let's clean out the infection so that it can heal. Help me to put the past where it belongs — in the past, over and done with.

—Anonymous

CRUCIFIXION, RESURRECTION

PRIEST AS NEXUS

PRIEST WITNESSES and proclaims that the universe is one. Yin and yang, life and death, male and female, good and evil, up and down, in and out, dark and light, flesh and spirit, matter and energy: all the polarities are one in God. The dying Christ hung precisely between a yes and a no.

A view of reality, religion, and morality that pits one-half of a duality or a polarity against the other (such as good versus evil, life versus death, light versus darkness, happiness versus sadness) is a harmful deception, a self-indulgent illusion, and a lie. Many popular and growing pseudo-religious movements are constructed around such self-indulgent illusions and lies; just beneath the surface lurks the dualistic deceptions and illusions of all the traditional forms of religions: us versus them, men versus women, rich versus poor, white versus black, spirit versus body, democracy versus communism, bliss versus suffering, so forth and so on.

Dualism in which partnerships of polarities are turned against each other is the land of either/or. Priest calls the people from the land of either/or into a new land, the land of both/and. Priest must never choose either the light or the dark as preferable to or better than the other. Priest is called to stand at the crossing, the nexus, the intersection of incompatible polarities and remain exactly there in the ripping tension, that witness can be made to the all-encompassing oneness of the divine. Priest surrenders easy solutions and comforting stability to proclaim that new and resurrected life is found exactly at the crossroad, in the midst of the agony and tension of the irreconcilable.

The Apple and the Needle

"As a small child, I had a recurring dream. It was for me a nightmare, terrifying in its sensations and in its repeated visitations. I dreamed I was standing and looking at my left hand and my right hand, both slightly outstretched. In the palm of my left hand was a long, polished, shiny, cold, incredibly sharp, incredibly thin, sewing needle. In the palm of my right hand was a large, round, luscious, red apple. Somehow, I knew that it was absolutely necessary for me to experience simultaneously both sensations of holding the apple and the needle. I was not to let either drop, nor was I to put the needle into the apple. I had to hold onto and feel the roundness and lusciousness and full-bodiedness in one hand and the thinness and coldness and sharpness and metalness in the other. The tension between the two sensations was almost unbearable. I was afraid I could not bear the intensity of the two. I was afraid I would literally be torn apart, ripped down the middle."

PRIEST AS DEATH'S FRIEND

THE CROSS is the preeminent symbol, an instrument of vicious execution, violent death. The broken and lifeless body of Jesus is dispensed as life food. The Way of the Cross is none other than the way of life. "Ye must die and be born again." The sacrifices of God are broken spirit and contrite heart. For life, all roads lead to death. Death is the most obvious and inevitable fact of our existence, and also, the most avoided and denied. In the presence of death, all of our rehearsed speeches of what we shall say and all our imagined scenarios of how it should go are rendered useless; we are called to be utterly present and surrender fully to the experience of the moment. In the presence of death, we can only embrace the one who embraces us. In the presence of death we are transformed; all transformations large or small require a dying. Death and her sisters — woundedness, failure, rejection, and suffering — are the magic ingredients, the necessary catalysts.

Priest has abundant life to proclaim, and none of it can be appreciated without death.

Priest must come to know death well, to know his or her own dyings well. Death is priest's given essential ingredient of the saving potion. Death is the indispensable ally. Without death, priest is fraud, a despicable charlatan. As death's friend, priest invites us to the edge of our abyss, urging us to topple in. Priest presides over the rituals of leaping and falling and dying, inviting us to know from that point on, it is all in God's hands. Priest introduces us to the practice of the presence of death. Priest's most familiar setting is at the pastoral edge of the abyss.

The Choice

Consider a man, mid-thirties, single, reaching ripeness in his chosen vocation as a writer. A year ago he took the AIDS test and discovered that he was HIV positive, or more exactly, HIV positive, asymptomatic. There were no signs of the ravaging disease. That set of circumstances made him eligible for a pilot research program in another state. So for nine months, he drove five hours, twice monthly, for physical check-ups and blood work while taking the prescribed dosage of the drug AZT. The purpose of the experimental program was to discover whether or not AZT, when administered at this very early stage of the disease, might have prophylactic capacities.

No symptoms appeared; however, he began to notice a steadying increase in his level of fatigue, along with an inability to think clearly or creatively. By the end of nine months, day in, day out, he felt horrible.

His blood work showed that he was severely anemic. All these are some of the possible side effects of AZT. Always feeling fatigued and ill was awful, but not being able to write was worse.

Two weeks ago, he made the decision to stop the AZT. Already, he feels much better. He is writing eagerly and creatively again, and looks forward to waking up in the morning. "The world has color again."

He assumes that his decision will cost him time; it will shorten his life. He has chosen for a more imminent death. He has reached out and embraced his mortality and by doing so has found his life restored.

The Deadly Assembly

The large, round clock, mounted high on the right wall of the auditorium, clicked nine o'clock as the last member of the senior class, filing in two by two, finally entered the hall. Tuesday morning assemblies housed the entire student body for a half hour of readings, announcements, and skits. Used by most students as a last opportunity to review vocabulary words, or read the last pages of an assignment, assemblies were instead supposed to be a time to express school spirit and community.

I will always remember the assembly of April 2, 1986, and the expression on the face of the director, Miss Wing — an expression with which only I could identify. This was the first assembly after March vacation. The procession was rather loud, voices rising above the notes of the piano, as the girls discussed their various experiences of vacation. Unfortunately, I was silent for the most part, occasionally responding to a "Hello" or a "What's up, Suse?" There was nothing of my March vacation that I wanted to discuss.

At the outset, my vacation had promised to be great. Two weeks of spring skiing in Vermont — what more could I ask for? Granted that many of my friends were in exotic places such as Europe or the Caribbean, I was perfectly content in my cozy Vermont ski house that rested on a ledge overlooking Mad River Glen. To enhance the trip, my twelve-year-old brother, Jake, and I were allowed to bring one friend each. We were both excited about skiing and just having fun.

I remember so vividly sitting around the yellow formica counter talking and recovering from a tough day on the slopes as my mother prepared dinner. Our conversation was interrupted by the bellow of our aged telephone. My father, who had gone home for two days to check on the condition of my cancer-stricken grandmother, was on the line. Excited to speak to Dad, we all grabbed for the phone that was perched between my mother's ear and her shoulder, since both hands were occupied stirring the rice and vegetables. We were anxious to report the events of the past two days — Jake's getting a gold in the NASTAR race and myself successfully completing the terror-filled trail, *Paradise*, for the first time. Mom quickly silenced us as we bickered over who would speak to Dad first. Her face became very solemn, and she freed her hands of the wooden spoons in order to hold the phone more securely. What was the matter? Why was Mom acting so strange?

By seven-fifteen the next morning the car was packed and Mom was draining the last hot water pipe. With moderate traffic we were sure to be home by eleven — just in time for early afternoon visiting hours. A car ride that was usually noisy with fighting over seat space and arguing about whether to eat at Burger King or McDonald's was silent.

Grandma's pancreatic cancer had intensified, spreading to her liver and giving her only days left to live. Both Jake and I were aware of the severity and probable outcome of cancer, but we never believed that it would get our grandmother. As we approached Whaleback Mountain, our two-hour marker, Jake began to cry and question my mother about Grandma's condition. I, on the other hand, just stared at the snow-covered hills out the frosty backdoor window.

I had been at Windsor for two and a half years. During these years my grandmother and I had grown closer and closer together. She, herself a Windsor graduate, prided herself that I was experiencing the same love and friendships that she once had. Windsor created a strong bond and intensified our grandmother/ granddaughter relationship. Trying out for the same athletic teams and having gotten involved in the student government as she once had, I realized that she had been a role model for me.

Pulling up in front of the Faulkner Hospital, my mother let us out to wait in the lobby as she looked for a convenient parking space. The elevator ride to the third floor seemed ever so quick to my nervous heart that was pounding at a rate of 130 pulses a minute and to my hands that were lubricated with my salty perspiration. I hesitated as I departed from the elevator door. I wasn't prepared to see my grandmother, a plump woman who loved to bake bread and cookies, lying helpless in bed, letting the cancer eat away at every cell in her body. I was scared of the woman whom I had so easily identified with and loved.

Having rejected the smallest piece of food, my body trembled with fatigue as I entered the first pew of St. Paul's Episcopal Church. Decorated in purple as it was holy week, the church was overflowing with sympathetic and saddened faces. By the second hymn, my Kleenex, which had felt like a rock under my leg at the opening of the ceremony, was nearly a crystal of sand. Grandma's funeral was the first time I had publicly expressed my emotions. I hadn't yet cried in front of my parents. Her casket, covered by a purple veil, lying in front of the altar, was the realization for me that my grandmother was truly dead.

I lived the five days after the funeral and before the return to school as any other days. I rarely found myself crying, and I basically didn't think about the loss of my grandmother. Occasionally I would yearn to talk and be with her, but I would force myself to quickly forget about her. Whether it was because I had matured or because I was just one of those people who keep things to themselves, I don't know.

Sitting next to Amy, my best friend, I became tense as Miss Wing greeted the students on their return from March break. As usual, she included something about her cat, Zander, and the need for students to take advantage of the last months between April and June to improve their grades. Then appeared the infamous yellow piece of paper. The one on which she always jotted little anecdotal stories or important announcements. Miss Wing, as she stood looking over the entire school from her position on the stage, possessed the same look that she had thrown me when I entered the assembly; I knew it was coming. My clammy hand grasped Amy's as Miss Wing began her tribute to my grandmother. Tears streamed down my face as Miss Wing announced the death of a most loyal and devoted alumna who had served on the alumnae association and was a dedicated grandmother to Susie in Class Five. To me the assembly hall was completely silent as Miss Wing continued her commendation of my grandmother; I could hear the click of the clock striking nine-thirty.

Exiting the auditorium, countless people patted me on the back or gave me a hug. Normally, I would have returned the gestures, but on that day I was so enveloped in the memories of my grandmother that I just walked out of the assembly hall without murmuring a word to anyone. I felt naked and inferior. Who was I? The entire school saw me crying, something that I had expressed only to my parents at the funeral; I felt so vulnerable. From now on I was just an ordinary Windsor girl. I only wish that my grandmother knew how I prided myself on being her granddaughter and attending a school that had so much respect for her, just as I did.

—Susie Dwinell

The Three Things

Every year
everything
I have ever learned
in my lifetime
leads back to this: the fires
and the black river of loss
whose other side
is salvation...
To live in this world
you must be able
to do three things:
to love what is mortal;
and to hold it
against your bones knowing

your own life depends on it;
and, when the time comes to let it go,
to let it go.

—Mary Oliver
in *American Primitive**

The Dying

She was remarkably old for a cat — twenty-two —
and she took a long time dying. Her name was Nicey.
Nicey came into my life nine years ago, when I married
Kathleen.

I was never a cat person. My father would not allow
cats in the house. My grandfather made sport of shoot-
ing them. We were definitely a dog family. So when
Nicey became a member of our new family, true to her
nature she singled me out as the person with whom she
would most closely bond.

Nicey and I became very good friends. She was
the most feline cat I have ever known — independent,
willful, savvy, determined, demanding, fiercely loyal,
beautiful, well groomed, autonomous, and every bit an
equal to humans. She liked me, chose me as the person
she wanted to be near, and whenever possible insisted
on my attention.

---

*Mary Oliver, *American Primitive*, p. 82.

It became clear about four years ago that her aging process had begun in earnest. She became less mobile. She started to lose weight. She slept more. And gradually her kidneys failed.

I will be forty-nine on my next birthday, and I am keenly aware of my aging process and my mortality. Increasingly, it becomes less a hypothetical issue and more and more a disturbing experiential fact. Having been on a rescue squad and having served as a parish priest, I have dealt with death. But I haven't dealt much with long-term aging and the *process* of dying.

Nicey aged and died with incredible dignity and spirit. She continued to delight in pleasure. She never once complained about her condition, and at the same time continued to insist on all her prerogatives within the family structure. Even as her body weakened, her presence seemed to strengthen.

The manner in which this cat, this twenty-two-year-old named Nicey, bore her aging and her dying offered a confrontation with my own mortality, and an instruction in what the quality of my own aging process might be for me.

This small creature who had chosen me changed me — in both my attitude toward death and my relationship with my own inevitable process of dying. Nicey the cat had priested *me*.

PRIEST AS KILLER

EACH OF US is born into the world with some essence, with some *self*, with archetypal reality and energy — energy that flows through the infant human organism as *eros* and vitality.

By the time most of us are six years old, we have learned that to be that archetypal self with openness and joy and enthusiasm is extraordinarily dangerous and places us in profound jeopardy. So by the age of six, each one of us has developed character armor. It is a personality, a network of defenses that serve to restrict the flow, to hide and protect the essential self from others and even from our own awareness. It does not take any of us very long to assume that this character armor, this set of defenses, this personality, is indeed our identity: thus we invest it with utter necessity.

As each of our lives unfolds and the years go by, the essential self insists on being known and being made manifest. It insists with louder and louder persistence. The essential self, that archetypal energy, is indeed of God, and God will not be denied. The eruption of God from within is that which we all fear, probably more than anything else, because it brings us face-to-face with the true self, which in the first six years of our lives we learned would bring fatal consequences. The horror for us all is that if the true self is not allowed out through the defenses, the consequences will likewise be fatal. God will not be denied.

The archetypal essence of each of us will make itself known even if it requires the damaging of the ego, the wounding or damaging of a human being's flesh, as in accident or disease, or finally even death.

What is fascinating is that in most cases the personality, the character armor, the defenses that we form and cling to are, in fact, the opposite of the deep self from which we are trying to protect ourselves. If people can identify their defenses, they can certainly find some very direct clues as to the archetypal nature of their beings; they can find some real directions regarding what destiny God has assigned them.

We know that God does not enter our lives through the easy path of least resistance. Rather, he enters through the unknown, the shadow, our blind spaces, the place where our defenses are the most thin. To be engaged by God is to be a volcano erupting; to be engaged by God is to be hit in the place where we are most vulnerable and thus most afraid.

Priest is someone who is willing to allow the struggle between the self and the personality (the struggle and journey toward authenticity and integrity) to be public. Priest is one who allows that struggle to be so public that it is a model and a witness and a proclamation for other human beings. Priest is one who models a willingness to allow God to break through, crash through, and kill personality, character armor, and defenses. To be priest is to willingly and publicly allow God to crucify the very things that we as a culture think are most precious. So priest is one who is willing to make public the personal Divine assassination. Priest is one who is often wounded and who knows the blessedness of wounding.

Priest is one who brings by presence, by word and by sacrament, the very weapons by which others' ego defenses, personality, and character armor will be attacked and destroyed. The integrity and authenticity of priest's struggle is not only an invitation and encouragement for others, but also just as certainly a threat and an attack. The word of scripture and the word of preaching are for comforting and inspiration; more important, if the word is to have any impact, it is an intrusion — an attack, an assault, a violation of the ego of the hearers. Moreover, if we understand sacraments fully, we will know that they are sources of nourishment to the soul. Yet to be sources of nourishment to the soul, they must likewise be violent to the ego. To baptize a person into the body of Christ is an act that contains all the violence and uprooting of grafting. To baptize someone into the death and resurrection of Christ is to baptize them into death and hell. To dispense the dismembered body of Jesus and the spilt blood of Jesus as the bread of heaven and the cup of salvation is nothing short of violence. Priest dispenses ticking time bombs. Priest is an attacker and killer of character armor, personality, and defenses.

The Inner Death

He shared the dream, thinking at first it was about nuclear war. He said, "I dreamed that I was in the woods and then in a house, and then walking from that house across a field to a bigger, older house. While I was in the middle of the field, the sky turned black like a line squall and came across the heavens at me and appeared all black and ferocious and with a terrible orange glow. I expected to be incinerated, but I wasn't. In fact, I felt nothing, no pain. After a while, I looked at my hand, and it began to blister and bubble and skin began to flake off, and I knew I was dying of radiation sickness." The dream image is of a man caught in the open, blasted by an incredible source of power, caught in an expectation of being overwhelmed and incinerated, but in reality, an inexorably internal process of change had begun. He experienced himself changed from the inside out in a way that everyone must notice. A mortal change, certainly a death of the self he thought he was, a flaking off of the old skin, the old cover, things bubbling up from inside out, a transformation, a death and rebirth. He thought he was going to die at the hands of an overwhelming external force, and what he found out was that he died at the hands of a slow, invisible, inexorable internal power.

—Ted Kaynor

The Lifeboat

The kingdom of heaven is like this:

A man awoke to find himself alone in a lifeboat. Everywhere he looked there was ocean. He was alone in the lifeboat and alone on the ocean. The lifeboat was stocked with food and water to last him many years.

As the days and nights went on, the man experienced and survived heat and cold, calm and storm, rain and blazing sun.

Although he survived, his life in his little craft was extremely monotonous, and his loneliness grew almost unbearable.

He began to pray. He prayed and prayed to God that he would be delivered. Nothing happened to change his life. He heard no answer to his prayer. He continued in his prayer.

Finally, one night, there was the voice of a father, "Leave your lifeboat." He could not believe his ears. Was this the answer to his prayers, to leave the boat?

He replied, "If I leave my lifeboat, I will surely die!" The father said, "You are already dying. Staying in the lifeboat is killing you. Leave! You must leave the lifeboat! Leave the boat, dive deep, and I will be waiting for you there."

The Rudder

During the summer of 1962 I was employed by Plymouth Yacht Club, Massachusetts, to run their summer sailing program. Late in the summer season the first hurricane of the year rolled in with 60– to 70–mile per hour winds and fairly heavy seas that wreaked havoc with the boat anchorage. During the storm a 45-foot power boat broke loose at the windward end of the anchorage and started moving through the moored boats, propelled by the wind.

In the spirit of the moment, another fellow and I boarded the errant craft with the intention of saving it and other boats in its way from harm. The other fellow, a mechanic at the local boatyard, said he would try to start the engine. I went up to the flying bridge and took the helm. With enough speed from the force of the wind, the boat had steerage way and I began to steer between the moored boats. It took a lot of effort, but by winding the wheel first one way, and then the other, I succeeded in missing boat after boat.

After several minutes my companion arrived on deck to announce he couldn't start the engine so would try to get the anchor over. Within minutes he had succeeded, and the boat was riding at anchor after a perilous but successful journey through the entire anchorage.

Later, when we were reviewing our heroic efforts, he told me that try as he might, he just couldn't connect the steering gear, so the steering wheel was never connected to the rudder! Thus, despite my valiant steering efforts, it was not I who steered that drifting craft successfully through all the others.

—Anonymous

PRIEST AS HUMILIATOR

IT IS A HARD FACT to come to terms with, but the truth is that in our culture, neglect, deprivation, and abuse are normative. So much so, in fact, that only the most egregious and perverted forms of abuse are able to attract our attention and arouse our passions. Sexual abuse, physical abuse, and psychological abuse abound — the statistics are endless. We abuse ourselves by allowing drunk driving to continue. We abuse ourselves by maintaining a penal system that turns out men and women who have become even more antisocial and violent. People who have been abused are made to feel ashamed. The capacity to absorb deprivation and abuse has been elevated into a virtue. Abuse is so commonplace that often when people are shown a situation in which they might not be abused, they are stunned and shocked.

Some forms of abuse are exceedingly subtle: asking a child to be the parent or to fill in some black hole in the parent's psyche; being raised in an alcoholic family; being forbidden to think certain thoughts or to have or express certain feelings; being shamed for creativity or curiosity. Or perhaps the most subtle form of abuse — emotional withholding. Abuse has come to be accepted as a normal part of life. We live in a Dark Age.

The opposite of and remedy for abuse is to be cherished and cherishing. Simply by virtue of his or her gift of life, every human being has the right to be cherished, and the obligation to cherish.

It is hard to swallow the reality of abuse. It is hard to admit that deprivation is part of the fabric of our culture, but even more difficult and painful to admit is our own collusion with abuse.

People raised in abusive families (or for that matter, people raised in an abusive culture) will not only come to perceive abuse as normal, but also, and even more devastating, will become abusers themselves. We come to accept the behavior of abuse. Sometimes that means we become overt abusers of others, either physically, or sexually, or emotionally, engaging in behaviors that society perceives as abusive. A more hidden form of abuse is self-abuse — emotional, psychological, physical. What does it take to break out of this hideous pattern of behavior?

Deep patterns of abuse blind us to who we really are in the fullness of our humanity. Breaking out of this hideous, self-defeating behavior requires being utterly grounded, brought to earth, set right down in the middle of our own crap and made to smell its stink. In the utter humiliation of my own existence I can be set free — by my own insight (if I am lucky enough), or when I can no longer stand my own pain, or when someone who cherishes me cares enough to puncture my self-denial and my disillusionment. I am able to look at the fact that I am the source of, the creator of, and the user and enjoyer of my own misery, and the source of the misery of others, I can release my addiction. If I can be humiliated badly enough, jolted hard enough, I may fall out of the lofty illusions, back to earth to become human again and thus be saved.

As Jesus' words and behaviors were often arrows that punctured inflated balloons and sacred cows — the illusions and denials of individuals and groups — and sent them hurtling toward the ground, likewise the calling of priest is, by virtue of words and deeds, to knock us out of orbit, blow us away, take the air out of our sails, puncture our balloons, and slaughter our sacred cows so that we may see who we really are and thus know what is available to us beyond who we really are. If I am not humiliated, I will never know cherishing. If someone doesn't care enough about me to show me how I abuse myself and how I abuse others, then I do not stand a chance of ever knowing what love is. We need to love and be loved, to be brought and to bring others to earth where God is — embarrassed, punctured, loved enough to be humiliated and reborn.

The Plunge

We are the children
Who never heard it
We are the children who never felt it

But we sensed it
With our bodies
And with our hearts
We sensed it
And ached for it
But our thoughts and our feelings
didn't
couldn't
Acknowledge it.
Shielded from Passion
We were damned to mediocrity
Good at what we do
But incapable
Of doing more
And life goes on . . .
Does it?
Is this life?
Is this "reasonable level-headedness" really It?
Shielded from Passion
We've been disabled
Part of our God-given humanity
Is bound
Like tiny feet
Pruned
Like Japanese trees.
Can we undo the damage?
Can we unwrap the gift?
Can those tiny feet learn to dance in the wind
And in doing so begin to grow?
Perhaps the answer is deep

Deep inside the hurts.
The deprivations.
But look!
I plunge!
Breaking the clear, placid surface
Sending splashing water and waves
As messengers to others.
And look!
I surface!
Carrying a barrel full of water
To keep as a reminder
Of the gift of pain.
In the depths of my pain
I am released!
Unwrapped!
Unbound!
I *feel*
Passionately!
And am now capable
Of love
Of reaching beyond mediocrity
Of reaching my full humanity!
Thank you God
For the courage
To plunge into pain

—Muriel Maybee

The Handshake

I am a student sitting at a desk in a class in Old English at the University of Southern Maine. I feel old to be sitting in a college classroom. Maybe because I am over 40.

This class is not what I expected. I first have to learn a new language called Old English. Most of the students in the class are considerably younger than I am. They seem to pick it up quicker than I do. This is a cause for a good amount of discomfort. The professor is very matter-of-fact. Seems to have little sense of humor. What is there to laugh about? I consider this very serious. It's my last class; I pick up language very slowly. I feel dumb in class. Dumb! What an embarrassment! I feel dumber than people half my age! What an outrage! I feel my face getting red whenever I open my mouth. I try to add, to question, to contribute in spite of feeling the rise of blood to my face. The professor turns away. He doesn't like to call on me, probably because of my red face, my utter discomfort, and I feel my body grow hot and the pores under my shirt open and I feel moist. At 43 I feel moist.

I feel the absolute humiliation I felt some 30 years ago when I was sitting in French class with Miss Soca. Miss Soca would call on me for an answer to a question in French and I was to respond in French. I couldn't understand the question, so how could I answer? I had

studied, but my mind was like a sieve. Some of my classmates had minds like sponges, and I was convinced I
was sitting in the middle of that classroom, an island
of ignorance with no way out, and Miss Soca was waiting, standing at the front of the room glaring at me to
answer the question. Finally, I would blurt out an answer. Anything. Anything to ease the terror from my
place in the middle of the room. The blood rose in Miss
Soca's face in response to my off-the-cuff, wild-guess
of an answer. Her lips drawn tight, she began in a
barely audible whisper to say ... what became louder
...and discernible ... and indescribable ... the words
forged in my brain like a hot iron. "Edouard, you
are so stupid. ... You stupid idiot, Edouard ... STUPID!
STUPID! STUPID!" ... and she nearly screamed the answer in French. But by then the terror of existence was
so overwhelming I couldn't understand. I was beyond
comprehension. The blood filled my head, steam from
the searing iron hissed from my brain and the work was
done; the message was implanted forever ... STUPID
... IDIOT!

And from my seat in the center of the room I could
feel wave upon wave of ignorance radiating out and in-
fecting the whole class. I was the cursed, the damned,
scum of the earth, scorched for life by the searing words
of Miss Soca, and I sat in the fire burning in pure damna-
tion, humiliation, at a time when I was a new student
in the school, the new kid in the class, fresh out of the
hills of Simsbury where King Philip stood and watched

the city burn from his cave atop the mountain, where I had sat in a police station at age 13 and faced up to my actions and took on full responsibility before the police chief in a confession of sordid sexual behavior propagated by a perverted older man and his perverted little dog. I had been plucked out of school by the police and placed on the hot seat in the station to make a full-blown complete confession of what this sordid man had told me and done to me, and later that evening I sat in the same station with my father and told the whole story over again.

In a moment I came of age. I was initiated into the world of men. I could speak, and my words carried weight. Here I was talking to my father and to a policeman. They listened; I saw respect in their eyes for what I was doing, and compassion for how difficult it was for me to say these words. They were true words spoken from the heart. I knew then what it was to speak the truth. I saw a vision of King Philip standing atop that mountain. He knew what it meant to speak the truth. As I finished my confession I stood up and felt I could hold my head up. I was ashamed of nothing; nothing had been hidden, and the police chief held out his hand, and I shook it. Through this difficult process I had been welcomed into the world of men.

On the way home I felt exhausted from the emptying of my heart; I felt drained but exhilarated because I had done what I knew was right — I felt initiated into the world of men. It was a test. I passed, and if King Philip were still standing at the mouth of the cave, he may have smiled slightly and nodded his approval because I was brave and maybe he would allow me into the brotherhood.

It was raining the night we left the police station. I rode in front next to my father, though in my mind, I have a picture of myself riding in the back seat, peering forward past the empty front seat at the windshield wiping away the rain. My father was silent. We both listened to the wipers banging back and forth on the windshield, and nothing was said. The world was crying and nothing was said. When would the brotherhood speak, when could we speak up and be heard, against child molesting, sexual harassment, racism, genocide, and poverty? Maybe it wasn't time yet. Maybe we had to wait for the intensity of the last day to be absorbed. My father would speak when the time was right, I was sure.

I don't remember how long I figured we would have to wait until something was said. I may have thought to myself, we would wait until we got home. But my mother would be there. Wasn't this talk to be among men? I didn't think my mother should be involved. She wouldn't understand. She was such a prude, anyway. Maybe my father would stop at a coffee shop, and we'd go in where it was warm and sit and talk together. I looked out the side window and saw the woods of Firetown Road and I knew we had passed all the shops of town. No, we wouldn't stop and have something to drink. Maybe my father would speak to me tomorrow, you know, about the brotherhood. He didn't.

I dropped the Old English Class.

—Ted Kaynor

PRIEST AS MONSTER

HOLY SPACES throughout the world, from culture to culture — temples, churches, ashrams, shrines — are adorned and guarded by carved statues, monsters, griffins, gargoyles, lions, dragons. The more horrific the representations of the monster, the better. The more ugly and frightening the beast, the more likely it is to appear guarding the entry to the holy space.

How are we to understand why the approaches to holy spaces are guarded by what appear to be the most unholy, the most demonic, the most grotesque? How can the ugly and monstrous defend and protect the holy? From what enemy do winged creatures with fangs and claws shield sanctified space?

The enemy is rationalism. Rationalism takes many forms: literalism, fundamentalism, trivialism, reductionism, cynicism, sentimentality. The enemy is rationalism in all its variations, for rationalism annihilates mystery, and holiness, and it destroys the power of the sacred to transform our lives, to crucify us, to resurrect us. Rationalism kills all symbolic power. It is against the rational parts of us that monsters stand guard. The more grotesque and irrational they appear, the more likely they are to confound and offend the rational in us and drive it away.

Symbolos, at the heart of the transforming mystery, is the dynamic of allowing fact after fact, experience after experience, to layer upon each other or to fall in upon each other, then looking at the totality and discerning all the levels of meaning, knowing that something potent is being revealed, something more potent even than the sum of all the parts.

Diabolos is the opposite of *symbolos*. It is the function of taking something apart into its separate pieces, of not allowing the collection of data or experience to resonate among those parts, to reduce paradox to simplicities, to reduce metaphor to literalism, to dilute meaning and vitality, to disturb the resonance of events so that mystery and revelation can occur.

It is to protect *symbolos*, and to guard against *diabolos*, that monsters surround spaces of holiness.

The word *monster* derives from the Latin word *monstare*, meaning to show forth, to warn, to demonstrate. Monsters show forth and demonstrate the *symbolos* power of the holy, and thus point to life at its deepest, indeed, point to the fact that life is deep upon deep.

Priest is, therefore, *symbolos*, a monster. Priest is one who "tells it like it is." Priest is one who does not trivialize or sentimentalize; priest is not cynical. Priest is one who bears witness to how bad things really are when they are bad, and how glorious things really are when they are glorious; how dead people are when they die; and how freshly alive people are when they are born. Priest says, "Let us look again, and again, and again," that "things are always more than they first appear. Let us always look under the surface to search for the hidden mystery even though it makes us most uncomfortable." Priest as monster guards against the diabolical nature of the rational to reduce everything to meaninglessness. Priest offends the literalness, the fundamentalness, the trivializing nature of the rational. Priest points to the reality that all space, inner and outer, is holy space. Priest is, therefore, a guardian of the sanctity of life. As the monstrosity of priest approaches, the boundaries expand and the levels increase, and the mystery deepens, and life is again vibrating with holiness.

The Exorcism

Transformation for me has come with bangs and also whimpers. The bangs I experienced when God first became real to me in 1974 at the age of 33. In a period of eight months, I changed from an alcoholic atheist to a sober believer in Jesus Christ. The whimpers of transformation have been slowly building inside of me ever since, so that imperceptibly I am changing from a self-hating scapegoat from an alcoholic family to a self-loving, yet suffering, pilgrim on a journey of exploration to experience what God means by the body of Christ.

I didn't ask God to reveal herself to me. She just did. One morning in the fall of 1973, I woke my husband, Reggie, and urged him to come with me. Reluctantly he

came, and we both had a compelling urge to continue
on successive Sundays. God-friends invited us to attend
a Sunday evening Bible study with other couples and
a charismatic Episcopal priest. We attended faithfully,
and I began reading the Bible and anything else I could
find about the natures of God and man.

In February of 1974, I had the strange experience
of waking up in the night believing I was a man who
intended to kill Reggie. I woke Reggie, told him, and
called the priest who was out of town. We made an
appointment as soon as he returned. I was convinced
I needed an exorcism. The exorcism was bland by the
standards I had read, but the transformational part was
fascinating to me and a turning point. The priest called
up many spirits such as lust and gluttony. Nothing
much happened, but when he called hate and asked
me whom I hated, I said glaringly to this man whom
I loved, "I hate you." At the onset of the exorcism, he
asked me if I believed in Jesus as my savior. I said I
thought Jesus was an important man and all, but that
his deity was freed.

In another meeting with a prayer group in the
priest's basement, I again felt myself to be a man. This
man was ugly and despicable to me. Silently I presented
him to God in fear, and I heard in my mind the words
of God saying to me, "I love that man." As I heard
the words, I felt my ribs mystically splitting open from
my sternum as if I were receiving the world into my
heart. The experience lasted for only a few seconds.
Then the ribs returned, protecting my heart from any

further penetration. Again I felt that when the monster was revealed, I was released to love.

In May of 1974, I went on retreat to a school of pastoral care in Hudson, New Hampshire, where I became aware of my dependence on alcohol and made a deal with God, stating that if she were real I'd depend on her instead of alcohol. With daily prayer, I haven't had a drink.

Then began the transformation by whimpers. I've spent many years of psychotherapy wondering if I would ever learn to dump depression and suicidal thoughts and when I would learn to trust — first myself, then my husband of twenty years, and close friends, to say nothing of life in general. The work has been slow and painstaking, involving therapy, AA, prayer, church groups, ACoA, daily meditations, lots of reading, graduate school, exercise, affirmations, a treatment center in South Dakota for adult children of alcoholics, many workshops, and the elimination of sugar, white flour, and caffeine. The most exciting change occurred on a vacation to Maui with my husband this month where, for the first time in twenty years, we were alone for ten days with no friends, no children, and no responsibilities. The vacation seemed to be a culmination of all of our efforts to learn to love each other. I had a sense, almost for the first time, of having a true companion and lover. I feel more vulnerable, but somehow safer.

I am growing to love the monster in me. God and my husband showed me he was lovable. With that base, I feel fairly safe in extending my trust to include a wider circle, believing we were created to be one body, each of us in Christ, none more important than the other, and all necessary to the healthy functioning of each part.

—Anonymous

The Troll

Dreamt I was at a castle or a fortress. I was Dr. McCoy of Star Trek, and I was with Spock. We were trying to secure the fortress. It seemed abandoned.

Damage, major damage, had been done to an internal door. There were sounds coming from deep in the castle. These sounded like feverish clanging and booming noises.

Anyway, we managed to reclose the inner door. I jumped and grabbed the edge or top of a huge mattress-like structure in the huge hall we stood in. I did this mostly out of a desire to get up off the floor and out of the way of whatever was coming out of the depths.

Next, I remember being with Superman. He, also, was working feverishly to close a door, only this was the main outer gate. We both had left the inner castle upon hearing the heavy booms, blows being levied against the inner door. We were retreating.

We sealed the boomers from the depths in the castle and moved up the canyon leading from the castle to the outside world. Here work had feverishly been done to forestall the advance of the unknown parties. There were huge ramparts blocking the way up and out.

Finally, the so-called enemy broke out of the castle. At their head stood a mysterious and very powerful troll-like creature which-who was known as the 5th Eldest and who had in this age never stepped out into the light of day. He shone like a golden monster troll-man. He definitely was possessed of magic. There was a sense that he served a master from the deep, that he was extremely powerful — even Superman had retreated — but that he might yet be defeated.

In the first battle fought hand to hand, there was no decisive outcome. The advance was not stopped, but the attack threatened to change the course of World History.

—Tom Chaplain

PRIEST AS ENEMY

JEREMIAH, agonizing that God had been part of his life from the very beginning and had brought him anguish and ruination, demanded that God get out of his life.

Moses said, "No, I will not go. No, I will not go."

Isaiah, pleading that he was a man of unclean lips, refused.

Peter, saying he was a sinner, balked.

Even Jesus in the garden wished that the cup should be taken from him.

All of them had been called by God, and all of them said, in some way, "No."

Each one of us is likewise summoned by God, and each one of us likewise in our own way says "No." Sometimes we say no by claiming that there hasn't been any call at all. Sometimes we say no by being just one of the boys. Sometimes we say no by becoming very religious, pious, and obsessed with righteousness and respectability. Sometimes we say no by assuming the posture of the overly humble and insinuating that God could not possibly choose such a one as we.

No matter how it is said, the "No" must be spoken.

The "No" must be spoken, for until we are able to say

"No," we can never say "Yes." Until we are able to say no and mean it, all of our yesses are mewling maybes.

Priest represents the call. The presence of priest raises the presence of vocation. Priest is the tangible and physical symbol against which the "No" may be (and often is) spoken. Priest embodies the power in the cosmos which demands our ultimate loyalty, and which inexorably threatens to invade and overturn our lives. God is a relentless force that will not withdraw until we have wrestled, struggled, and spoken the "No," and then with our hearts broken, finally said the "Yes." To see priest is to behold the total disruption of our life, to behold the one with whom we must struggle, contend, resist, and to whom we must say "No."

The Bull's Eye

Ask people to give an example of religious rigidity, and in all likelihood, they could readily cite several. Religious rigidity is universal, coming in all sizes and shapes and covering the entire spectrum of religious expression.

Each of us is, of course, most likely to be highly aware of someone else's religious rigidity while at the same time being blind to our own.

While acknowledging the full extent of the vicious and brutal damage and destruction done in service of religious rigidity, at the same time we must understand that it is also a grace-filled gift.

Every single one of us (none of us escapes) comes to a place or places on our spiritual pilgrimage when our way of doing things fails. God on our terms as we know God is no longer adequate. All the inner images of God that once were full of authority and meaning and gave order to our universe simply no longer have vitality or sacredness. Familiar and treasured forms of worship, prayer, and other spiritual practices suddenly bottom out and become hollow and shallow. God *my* way, God on *my* terms, is simply being outgrown. It is a time of terrible loss, of confusion, of agony and despair and rage. It is the dark night of the soul. In those moments, we stand on the edge of the abyss and stare into the vastness of nothingness (no thing ness). If we can bear and tolerate this moment of crucifixion, the prize will be a new knowing of God, or, rather, God as God on God's terms, knowing us — a radically expanded and deepened spiritual universe.

But if, on the other hand, the terror, the loss and the fear of the unknown abyss is too much, we will retreat from the edge and regress back into a former way of knowing, loving, and worshipping God. We will then hold on with clenched fists. Our fear and our terror will set like wet cement and we will become increasingly rigid. We then move from being quarrelsome, annoying, and irritating toward becoming theological and religious bullies.

No matter how obnoxious a person or a group is in this religious rigidity, we must remember that the rigidity is not primarily motivated by the desire to control other people; rather, it is primarily motivated by the desire to control God, for the fear that so profoundly constellates religious rigidity is the fear of God. Religious rigidity is denial: denial of God, denial of the unknown God. Rigidity in the name of God is actually a defense against God.

If one wants to know precisely where God is attempting to break through into one's life, one only has to look at one's own religious rigidity. It doesn't matter what form rigidity takes — whether it is biblical fundamentalism, or liturgical preciousness. It is still the symptom of the clash or our need to have God on our terms, and God's need to have us know him/her/them on his/her/their terms.

Each of us could use our own religious rigidity as a sure and certain guide to knowing exactly where God is making contact and is pounding in. If we can thus use those fear-frozen rigid places in us as windows of discernment, they then become grace-filled sacraments.

PRIEST AS HUMOR

WHAT DOES IT MEAN to laugh? to tell jokes? to be humorous? to watch comedy? And how is it that all of us human beings find the joke, the comedy, the laugh, so intriguing, so compelling, so powerfully refreshing?

This uniquely human capacity must have within it some aspect of the divine to occupy such a central and powerful place in the human experience. When someone tells a joke, urges us to laugh, ushers us into the realm of comedy, we are, in fact, being invited to alter our perspective, or better yet, to change our standpoint — that place beneath us where we plant our feet, the ground of our being from which we speak and out of which come our values and for which we are often willing to fight and even to die.

Being invited to move or alter our worldview is no small thing; rather, it can be quite provocative, and even perhaps inflammatory. Yet humor, while it often provokes, does not often inflame. It can, in fact, soothe and relax.

How often we find ourselves in tense or sticky situations with both feet firmly planted, squarely confronting another or others who are likewise firmly rooted. Seemingly there is no way out, other than disagreement, conflict, rupture, fragmentation.

And then someone tells a joke, creates humor, and miraculously, the frozenness of the situation is broken and there seems to be maneuvering room, fresh air to breathe; people's bodies relax. What has happened?

Humor always requires a person to take a view of a situation from outside that situation. The perspective has to be one of an outside observer, stepping out or back far enough to see a situation in its absurdity. To tell the joke and to get the joke requires that at least one foot be moved, so that while we may have one foot still firmly planted at the original point, the other foot has moved to ground outside the originally defined situation. And now, it is from that other ground of being that the new perspective can be shared and the humor and absurdity of the original situation can be perceived.

Humor thus always offers another reality, and if there can be one reality beyond the original given reality, then, in fact, there are an infinite number of possible realities. In humor, we are relieved of the theological error of taking any reality as the ultimate one. And we are relieved of taking ourselves seriously. In humor, one foot stays planted on the original space, but the other has moved to a new place. And where is that new place and what is it made of? And who put it there? Is it perhaps the ever-present grace of God that provides that alternative space upon which to plant a foot anew and from which to re-view the situation?

Humor frees us thus from our self-imposed idolatries and rigidity. Humor gives us an instant firsthand experience of the grace and mercy of God. There is always more than one way of looking at something. We mortals are not stuck in our own limited and myopic perceptions. Humor is one of God's greatest inventions.

The Red Nose

In my left pocket I always carry a red plastic clown's nose. I've done it for years. I do it because it's fun on occasion to slip it on my nose and watch the profound impact that the red nose of inebriation has on people. The clowning of spiritual drunkenness is transformative.

It was a very hot and humid summer evening in Portland, Maine, and my wife and I had gone to a local movie theater for an 8:30 P.M. movie. When we arrived, we found the lobby already quite full. Several local summer camps had given their male counselors the evening off, so the lobby was populated by approximately 200 young men who had been cooped up for weeks with their charges and were looking for a fun-filled respite. As the non-air-conditioned lobby became even more crowded, the humidity and heat rose, and an ominous tension began to seep around.

There was only one ticket taker, a somewhat shy teenage girl, and for some reason, seating for the movie had to be delayed. The tension grew. There were slightly off-color jokes, and then the jokes became more and more overtly sexual. The young woman grew increasingly nervous and afraid. Not only was being in the lobby becoming quite unpleasant, it had all the makings of developing into a dangerous situation.

I decided to put on my nose. And so I did. With my nose on, I simply wandered around the lobby, looking at no one in particular, but observing the rug and the ceiling and the popcorn machine. The effect was instantaneous and marvelous. People began to chuckle and laugh out loud and the whole room relaxed. The young girl felt safe; nothing bad was going to happen, after all.

EPILOGUE

WE SHALL NEVER fully penetrate the mystery of priest. We shall never see fully into the jewel. We shall never fully discern the totality of priest.

However, the images that are reflected from each facet of the jewel are like the tracks of an animal. By noticing, by taking in, by tracking priest image by image, clue by clue, we may never come to see priest fully. But better yet, instead of seeing fully, we in fact become priest from the inside out. As priest dispenses wafer and wine — the tracks of God — we, by eating and drinking, even though we cannot see God fully, become more and more fully God. Likewise, by taking in the partial images of priest, we become priest. May we continue the tracking.

"The Tracker"

"The first track is the end of the string. At the far end, a being is moving, a mystery, dropping a hint about itself every so many feet, telling you more and more and more about itself until you can almost see it, even before you come to it. The mystery reveals itself slowly track by track, giving its genealogy early to coax you in. Further on, it will tell you the intimate details of its life and work, until you know the make of the track like a life-long friend.

"The mystery leaves itself like a trail of bread-crumbs, and by the time your mind has eaten its way to the maker of the tracks, the mystery is inside of you, part of you forever. The tracks of every mystery ever swallowed move inside your own tracks, shading them with nuances that show you how much more you have become than what you were. Man goes through the world eating his mysteries."*

---

*Tom Brown, Jr., *The Tracker*, p. 9.

Jesus

He said, "Do not call me good."

He fled when they came to make him King.

He said, "You sister, and you brother, shall do as I have
   done and greater things still."

He washed feet.

But hear him, we will not.
We will have our convenience — to elevate him,
   to set him so far above,
To grovel before him in self-indulgent humility,
Refusing to see ourselves as he sees us.
And so, the whole thing is perverted.
   He bleeds and bleeds and bleeds.
   We break his heart,
   and he weeps and bleeds and bleeds.

APPENDIX

For the reader interested in exploring the use and understanding of the concept of priest in the Old and New Testaments, the following biblical citations are offered for your investigation (based largely on *Strong's Exhaustive Concordance of the Bible*, by James Strong, S.T.D., LL.D., Abingdon Press, New York, 1974).

Entry: **Priest,** Old Testament occurrences

Genesis
14:18	was the priest of the most high God
41:45	daughter of Potipherah priest of Heliopolis
46:20	of Potipherah priest of Heliopolis bore to

Exodus
2:16	priest of Midian had seven daughters
3:1	father in law, the priest of Midian
18:1	Jethro, the priest of Midian, Moses'
29:30	that son that is priest in his stead
31:10	holy garments for Aaron the priest
35:19	holy garments for Aaron the priest
38:21	Ithamar, son to Aaron the priest
39:41	holy garments for Aaron the priest

Leviticus
1:7	Aaron the priest shall put fire upon the
9	the priest shall burn all on the altar

12	priest shall lay them in order on the
13	priest shall bring it all, and burn it
15	the priest shall bring it to the altar
17	the priest shall burn it on the altar
2:2	priest shall burn the memorial of it
8	when it is presented to the priest
9	priest shall take from the meal offering
16	the priest shall burn the memorial of it
3:11	the priest shall burn it on the altar
16	priest shall burn them on the altar
4:3	priest who is anointed sins according
5	priest who is anointed shall take of the
6	priest shall dip his finger in the blood
7	priest shall put some of the blood on
10	priest shall burn them on the altar
16	priest who is anointed shall bring of
17	priest shall dip his finger in some of
20	the priest shall make an atonement for
25	the priest shall take of the blood of the
26	priest shall make an atonement for him
30	priest shall take of the blood thereof
31	priest shall make an atonement for him
34	priest shall take of the blood of the sin
35	priest shall burn them on the altar
35	priest shall make an atonement for his
5:6	priest shall make an atonement for him
8	shall bring them to the priest who
10	priest shall make an atonement for him
12	Then shall he bring it to the priest and
12	the priest shall take his handful of it
13	priest shall make an atonement for him
16	priest shall make an atonement for him
18	for a guilt offering, to the priest
18	priest shall make an atonement for him
6:6	for a guilt offering, to the priest
7	priest shall make an atonement for him
10	priest shall put on his linen garment

12	the priest shall burn wood on it every
22	the priest of his sons who is anointed
23	offering for the priest shall be wholly
26	The priest who offers it for sin shall
7:5	priest shall burn them on the altar
7	the priest who makes atonement
8	priest who offers any man's burnt
8	priest shall have to himself the skin
31	priest shall burn the fat on the altar
32	you shall give to the priest as an offering
34	to Aaron the priest and to his sons
12:6	she shall bring to the priest
8	priest shall make an atonement for her
13:2	shall be brought to Aaron the priest
3	priest shall look on the plague in the
3	priest shall look on him, and pronounce
4	priest shall shut up him that has the
5	priest shall look on him the seventh
6	the priest shall look on him again the
6	the priest shall pronounce him clean
7	that he has been seen of the priest for
7	he shall be seen of the priest again
8	if the priest see that, behold, the scab
8	priest shall pronounce him unclean
9	he shall be brought to the priest
10	And the priest shall see him: and,
11	priest shall pronounce him unclean
12	foot wherever the priest looks;
13	Then the priest shall consider: and
15	the priest shall see the raw flesh, and
13:16	white, he shall come to the priest;
17	And the priest shall see him: and,
17	the priest shall pronounce him clean
19	reddish, and it be shown to the priest
20	when the priest sees it, behold, it be
20	priest shall pronounce him unclean:
21	if the priest look on it, and, behold

21	priest shall shut him up seven days
22	the priest shall pronounce him unclean
23	the priest shall pronounce him clean.
25	the priest shall look upon it: and
25	priest shall pronounce him unclean
26	if the priest look on it, and, behold
26	priest shall shut him up seven days
27	priest shall look upon him the seventh
27	priest shall pronounce him unclean
28	the priest shall pronounce him clean:
30	the priest shall see the plague and
30	priest shall pronounce him unclean
31	priest look on the plague of the scall,
31	priest shall shut up him that has the
32	the priest shall look on the plague:
33	priest shall shut up him that has the
34	day the priest shall look on the scall
34	the priest shall pronounce him clean
36	priest shall look on him: and, behold,
36	priest shall not seek for yellow hair;
37	the priest shall pronounce him clean
39	Then the priest shall look: and, behold,
43	priest shall look upon it: and, behold,
44	the priest shall pronounce him utterly
49	and shall be shown to the priest:
50	the priest shall look upon the plague
53	if the priest shall look, and, behold, the
54	priest shall command that they wash
55	And the priest shall look on the plague,
56	And if the priest look, and, behold, the
14:2	He shall be brought to the priest
3	priest shall go forth out of the camp;
3	priest shall look, and, behold, if the
4	the priest command to take for him
5	priest shall command that one of the
11	the priest who makes him clean shall
12	the priest shall take one he lamb, and

14	the priest shall take some of the blood
14	priest shall put it on the tip of the
15	priest shall take some of the log of oil,
16	the priest shall dip his right finger in
17	the priest put upon the tip of the right
18	the priest shall make an atonement for
19	priest shall offer the sin offering, and
20	the priest shall offer the burnt offering
20	priest shall make an atonement for him
23	day for his cleansing to the priest
24	the priest shall take the lamb of the
24	the priest shall wave them for a wave
25	the priest shall take some of the blood
26	priest shall pour of the oil into the palm
27	the priest shall sprinkle with his right
28	the priest shall put of the oil that is in
31	priest shall make an atonement for him
35	shall come and tell the priest saying,
36	the priest shall command that they
36	before the priest go into it to see the
36	the priest shall go in to see the house
38	the priest shall go out of the house to
39	the priest shall come again the seventh
40	the priest shall command that they
44	the priest shall come and look, and
48	if the priest shall come in, and look
48	priest shall pronounce the house clean,
15:14	and give them to the priest
15	the priest shall offer them, the one for
15	priest shall make an atonement for him
29	pigeons, and bring them to the priest
30	the priest shall offer the one for a sin
30	the priest shall make an atonement
16:30	shall the priest make an atonement for
32	the priest whom he shall anoint, and
17:5	to the priest, and offer them for
6	and the priest shall sprinkle the blood

19:22	priest shall make an atonement for him
21:9	daughter of any priest, if she profane
10	the high priest among his brethren,
21	blemish of the seed of Aaron the priest
22:10	a sojourner of the priest, or a hired
11	if the priest buy any soul with his
14	it to the priest with the holy thing
23:10	first fruits of harvest to the priest
11	the sabbath the priest shall wave it
20	the priest shall wave them with the
20	shall be holy to the Lord for the priest
27:8	shall present himself before the priest
8	the priest shall value him; according
8	that vowed shall the priest value him
11	present the beast before the priest
12	the priest shall value it, whether it be
12	who is the priest, so shall it be
14	the priest shall estimate it, whether it
14	the priest shall estimate it, so shall it
18, 23	the priest shall reckon to him the

Numbers

3:6	present them before Aaron the priest
32	Eleazar the son of Aaron the priest
4:16	of Eleazar the son of Aaron the priest
28, 33	Ithamar the son of Aaron the priest
5:8	even to the priest; beside the ram of
9	which they bring to the priest shall
10	whatever any man gives the priest
15	the man bring his wife to the priest
16	the priest shall bring her near, and set
17	the priest shall take holy water in an
17	and of the dust ... the priest shall take
18	the priest shall set the woman before
18	priest shall have in his hand the bitter
19	the priest shall charge her by an oath
21	priest shall charge the woman with an

5:21	the priest shall say to the woman
23	the priest shall write these curses in a
25	the priest shall take the jealousy offering
26	the priest shall take a handful of the
30	priest shall apply to her all this
6:10	or two young pigeons, to the priest
11	the priest shall offer the one for a sin
16	priest shall bring them before the Lord
17	priest shall offer also his meat offering
19	priest shall take the sodden shoulder
20	the priest shall wave them for a wave
20	this is holy for the priest with the wave
7:8	of Ithamar the son of Aaron the priest
15:25	priest shall make an atonement for all
28	priest shall make an atonement for the
16:37	Eleazar the son of Aaron the priest
39	Eleazar the priest took the brasen
18:28	give offering to Aaron the priest
19:3	shall give her to Eleazar the priest
4	And Eleazar the priest shall take of her
6	the priest shall take cedar wood, and
7	Then the priest shall wash his clothes
7	priest shall be unclean until the even
25:7	the son of Aaron the priest saw it, he
11	son of Aaron the priest has turned
26:1	Eleazar the son of Aaron the priest
3	and Eleazar the priest spoke with them
63	by Moses and Eleazar the priest who
64	Moses and Aaron the priest numbered
27:2	Moses, and before Eleazar the priest
19	And set him before Eleazar the priest
21	he shall stand before Eleazar the priest
22	and set him before Eleazar the priest
31:6	Phinehas the son of Eleazar the priest
12	to Moses, and Eleazar the priest and
13	Moses, and Eleazar the priest and all
21	Eleazar the priest said to the men of

26	and Eleazar the priest and the chief
29	give it to Eleazar the priest for an
31	and Eleazar the priest did as the Lord
41	to Eleazar the priest as the Lord
51, 54	and Eleazar the priest took the gold
32:2	to Moses, and to Eleazar the priest
28	Moses commanded Eleazar the priest
33:38	the priest went up into Mount Hor at
34:17	Eleazar the priest and Joshua the son
35:25	in it until the death of the high priest
28	until the death of the high priest
28	after the death of the high priest, the
32	the land, until the death of the priest

Deuteronomy

17:12	will not listen to the priest who
18:3	shall give to the priest the shoulder
20:2	priest shall approach and speak to
26:3	you shall go to the priest who shall
4	priest shall take the basket out of your

Joshua

14:1	which Eleazar the priest and Joshua
17:4	came near before Eleazar the priest
19:51	which Eleazar the priest and Joshua
20:6	until the death of the high priest that
21:1	the Levites to Eleazar the priest
4	the children of Aaron the priest, which
13	gave to the children of Aaron the priest
22:13	Phinehas the son of Eleazar the priest
30	And when Phinehas the priest and the
31	the son of Eleazar the priest said to
32	Phinehas the son of Eleazar the priest

Judges

17:5	one of his sons, who became his priest
10	and be to me a father and a priest

12	the young man became his priest and
13	seeing I have a Levite to my priest
18:4	and has hired me, and I am his priest
6	priest said to them, Go in peace:
17	priest stood in the entering of the gate
18	said the priest to them, What are you doing?
19	us, and be to us a father and a priest
19	be a priest to a tribe and a family in
24	my gods which I made, and the priest
27	had made, and the priest which he had

I Samuel

1:9	Now Eli the priest sat on a seat by a
2:11	to the Lord, before Eli the priest
14	the fleshhook brought up the priest took
15	Give flesh to roast for the priest for
28	all the tribes of Israel to be my priest
35	And I will raise me up a faithful priest
14:3	son of Eli, the Lord's priest in Shiloh
19	while Saul talked to the priest that
19	Then said the priest, Let us draw near
21:1	David to Nob to Ahimelech the priest
2	David said to Ahimelech the priest
4	the priest answered David, and said,
5	David answered the priest, and said
6	So the priest gave him hallowed bread
9	the priest said, The sword of Goliath
22:11	king sent to call Ahimelech the priest
23:9	he said to Abiathar the priest, Bring
30:7	And David said to Abiathar the priest

II Samuel

15:27	king said also to Zadok the priest

I Kings

1:7	and with Abiathar the priest: and
8	But Zadok the priest and Benaiah the

19	of the king, and Abiathar the priest
25	of the host, and Abiathar the priest
26	me your servant, and Zadok the priest
32	David said, Call me Zadok the priest
34	let Zadok the priest and Nathan the
38	So Zadok the priest and Nathan the
39	Zadok the priest took a horn of oil out
42	the son of Abiathar the priest came:
44	with him Zadok the priest and Nathan
45	And Zadok the priest and Nathan the
2:22	for him, and for Abiathar the priest
26	to Abiathar the priest said the king
27	banished Abiathar from being priest
35	Zadok the priest did the king put in the
4:2	Azariah the son of Zadok the priest

II Kings

11:9	that Jehoiada the priest commanded
9	and came to Jehoiada the priest
10	did the priest give King David's spears
14	Jehoiada the priest commanded the
15	priest had said, Let her not be killed in
18	killed Mattan the priest of Baal before
18	priest appointed officers over the house
12:2	Jehoiada the priest instructed him
7	Jehoash called for Jehoiada the priest
9	Jehoiada the priest took a chest and
10	scribe and the high priest came up
16:10	the priest the fashion of the altar
11	And Urijah the priest built an altar
11	Urijah the priest made it against King
15	Ahaz commanded Urijah the priest
16	Thus did Urijah the priest according
22:4	Go up to Hilkiah the high priest that
8	And Hilkiah the high priest said to
10	the priest has given me a book
12	king commanded Hilkiah the priest

14	so Hilkiah the priest and Ahikam and
23:4	commanded Hilkiah the high priest
24	the book that Hilkiah the priest found
25:18	the guard took Seraiah the chief priest
18	Zephaniah the second priest and the

I Chronicles

16:39	Zadok the priest, and his brethren the
24:6	the princes, and Zadok the priest and
27:5	the son of Jehoiada, a chief priest
29:22	chief governor, and Zadok to be priest

II Chronicles

13:9	be a priest of them that are no gods
15:3	without a teaching priest and without
19:11	Amariah the chief priest is over you in
22:11	the wife of Jehoiada the priest (for she
23:8	Jehoiada the priest had commanded
8	Jehoiada the priest dismissed not the
9	Jehoiada the priest delivered to the
14	Jehoiada the priest brought out the
14	For the priest said, Do not put her to death
17	killed Mattan the priest of Baal before
24:2	all the days of Jehoiada the priest
20	the son of Jehoiada the priest which
25	of the sons of Jehoiada the priest
26:17	Azariah the priest went in after him
20	And Azariah the chief priest and all
31:10	Azariah the chief priest of the house of
34:9	they came to Hilkiah the high priest
14	Hilkiah the priest found a book of the
18	the priest has given me a book

Ezra

2:63	till there stood up a priest with Urim
7:5	the son of Aaron the chief priest
11	Artaxerxes gave to Ezra the priest

12	to Ezra the priest a scribe of the
21	whatever Ezra the priest the scribe
8:33	Meremoth the son of Uriah the priest
10:10	Ezra the priest stood up, and said to
16	Ezra the priest with certain chief of

Nehemiah

3:1	high priest rose up with his brethren
20	the house of Eliashib the high priest
7:65	till there stood up a priest with Urim
8:2	Ezra the priest brought the law before
9	and Ezra the priest the scribe and the
10:38	priest the son of Aaron shall be with
12:26	and of Ezra the priest, the scribe
13:4	before this, Eliashib the priest having
13	the treasuries, Shelemiah the priest
28	the son of Eliashib the high priest

Psalms

110:4	are a priest forever after the order of

Isaiah

8:2	witnesses to record, Uriah the priest
24:2	as with the people, so with the priest
28:7	the priest and the prophet have erred

Jeremiah

6:13	from the prophet even to the priest
8:10	from the prophet even to the priest
14:18	and the priest go about into a land
18:18	the law shall not perish from the priest
20:1	Pashur the son of Immer the Priest
21:1	the son of Maaseiah the priest, saying
23:11	both prophet and priest are profane
33	the prophet, or a priest, shall ask you
34	the priest and the people, who shall
29:25	son of Maaseiah the priest and to all

26	The Lord has made you priest in the
26	in the stead of Jehoiada the priest
29	Zephaniah the priest read this letter in
37:3	the son of Maaseiah the priest to the
52:24	the guard took Seraiah the chief priest
24	and Zephaniah the second priest and

Lamentations

2:6	of his anger the king and the priest
20	the priest and the prophet be killed in

Ezekiel

1:3	came expressly to Ezekiel the priest
7:26	the law shall perish from the priest
44:13	to do the office of a priest to me
21	Neither shall any priest drink wine
22	or a widow that had a priest before
30	to the priest the first of your dough
45:19	priest shall take of the blood of the sin

Hosea

4:4	are as they who strive with the priest
6	that you shall be no priest to me
9	there shall be, like people, like priest

Amos

7:10	the priest of Beth-el sent to Jeroboam

Haggai

1:1, 12, 14	son of Josedech, the high priest
2:2	the son of Josedech, the high priest
4	son of Josedech, the high priest

Zechariah

3:1	he showed me Joshua the high priest
8	Hear now, O Joshua the high priest

| 6:11 | the son of Josedech, the high priest |
| 13 | he shall be a priest upon his throne |

Entry: **Priest,** New Testament occurrences

Matthew

8:4	show yourself to the priest and offer
26:3	to the palace of the high priest who
57	him away to Caiaphas the high priest
62	and the high priest arose and said to
63	and the high priest answered and said to
65	Then the high priest tore his clothes

Mark

1:44	show yourself to the priest and offer for
2:26	in the days of Abiathar the high priest
14:47	struck a servant of the high priest and
53	they led Jesus away to the high priest
14:54	even into the palace of the high priest
60	the high priest stood up in the midst
61	Again the high priest asked him and
63	Then the high priest tore his clothes
66	one of the maids of the high priest

Luke

1:5	a certain priest named Zacharias of
5:14	and show yourself to the priest and offer
10:31	there came down a certain priest that
22:50	struck the servant of the high priest

John

11:49	being the high priest that same year
51	but being high priest that year, he
18:13	was the high priest that same year
15	disciple was known to the high priest

15	Jesus into the palace of the high priest
16	which was known to the high priest
19	the high priest then asked Jesus of his
22	Is that how you answer the high priest?
24	him bound to Caiaphas the high priest
26	One of the servants of the high priest

Acts

4:6	Annas the high priest and Caiaphas
6	were of the family of the high priest
5:17	Then the high priest rose up and all
21	But the high priest came and they that
24	the high priest and the captain of the
27	council: and the high priest asked them
7:1	Then said the high priest, Are these
9:1	of the Lord, went into the high priest
14:13	Then the priest of Jupiter, Which was
22:5	the high priest can bear me witness
23:2	the high priest Ananias commanded
4	said Revilest thou God's high priest?
5	brethren, that he was the high priest?
24:1	Ananias the high priest descended with
25:2	high priest and the chief of the Jews

Hebrews

2:17	a merciful and faithful high priest in
3:1	and High Priest of our profession
4:14	then that we have a great high priest
15	For we do not have a high priest who
5:1	every high priest taken from among
5	not himself to be made a high priest
6	You are a priest forever after the
10	of God a high priest after the order of
6:20	made a high priest forever after the
7:1	priest of the most high God, who met
3	of God; remains a priest continually
11	priest should rise after the order of

15	of Melchizedek...arises another priest
17	You are a priest forever after the
20	not without an oath he was made priest
21	You are a priest forever after the
26	such a high priest became us, who is
8:1	We have such a high priest, who is set
3	For every high priest is ordained to
4	on earth, he should not be a priest
9:7	went the high priest alone once every
11	But Christ being come a high priest of
25	high priest enters into the holy place
10:11	priest stands daily ministering and
21	a high priest over the house of God
13:11	sanctuary by the high priest for sin

Entry: **Priesthood,** Old Testament occurrences

Exodus
| 40:15 | shall surely be an everlasting priesthood |

Numbers
16:10	with you: and you seek the priesthood also?
18:1	shall bear the iniquity of your priesthood
25:13	the covenant of an everlasting priesthood

Joshua
| 18:7 | priesthood of the Lord is their inheritance |

Ezra
| 2:62 | they, as polluted, put from the priesthood |

Nehemiah
7:64	they, as polluted, put from the priesthood
13:29	because they have defiled the priesthood
29	and the covenant of the priesthood and of

— ◊ —

Entry: **Priesthood,** New Testament occurrences

Hebrews

7:5	who receive the office of the priesthood
11	perfection were by the levitical
12	For the priesthood being changed, there is
14	Moses spoke nothing concerning priesthood
24	ever, has an unchangeable priesthood

I Peter

2:5	up a spiritual house, a holy priesthood
9	a chosen generation, a royal priesthood

— ◊ —

Hebrew and Greek Meanings of the Original Words Used

Entry #	Original Meaning
3548	**kohene;** *ko-hane'* act. part. of 3547; lit. one *officiating*, a *priest;* also (by courtesy) an *acting priest* (although a layman):-chief ruler, X own, priest, prince, principal officer
3549	**kahen;** (Chald.) *kaw-hane',* corresp to 3548: - priest
3547	**kahan;** *kaw-han';* a prim. root, appar. mean. to *mediate* in religious services; but used only as denom. from 3548; to *officiate* as a priest; fig. to *put on regalia:* - deck, be (do the office of a, execute the, minister in the) priest ('s office).

2409	**chattaya** (Chald.), *Khat-taw-yaw'*; from the same as 2408; *an expiation:* - sin offering
749	**'arak** (Chald.), *ar-ak'*; prop. corresp. to 748, but used only in the sense of *reaching to* a given point; to *suit* - be meet.
748	**'arak** *aw'rak'*; a prim. root; to be (caus. *make*)*long* (lit. or fig.): - defer, draw out, lengthen, (be, become, make pro-) long + (out, over-) live, tarry (long).
3550	**kehunnah**, *keh-hoon-naw'*; from 3547; *priesthood:* - priesthood, priest's office
2405	**iepateia hierateia,** *hee-er-at-i'-ah;* from 2407; *priestliness,* i.e. the *sacerdotal function:* office of the priesthood, priest's office
2420	**iepwosun hierosune** *hee-er-o-soo'-nay;* from 2413; *sacredness,* i.e. (by impl.) the *priestly office:* - priesthood.
2406	**iepateuma hierateuma,** *hee-er-at'yoo-mah;* from 2407; the *priestly fraternity,* i.e. a *sacerdotal order* (fig.): - priesthood

BIBLIOGRAPHY

Avens, Robert. *Imagination Is Reality*. Dallas: Spring Publications, 1980.

Berger, Peter. *The Precarious Vision*. New York: Doubleday & Company, 1961.

Borg, Marcus. *Jesus, A New Vision*. New York: Harper & Row, 1987.

Bornkamm, Gunther. *Jesus of Nazareth*. San Francisco: Harper & Row, 1960.

Brown, Tim, Jr. *The Tracker*. New York: Berkley Publishing, 1982.

Buckley, Michael. "Because Beset with Weakness," *To Be A Priest*, ed. by Robert E. Terwilliger and Urban T. Hoklmes III. New York: Seabury Press, 1975.

Edinger, Edward. *The Christian Archetype*. Toronto: Inner City Books, 1987.

————. *Encounter with the Self: William Blake's Illustrations of the Book of Job*. Toronto: Inner City Books, 1986.

Fox, Matthew. *Meditations with Meister Eckhart*. Santa Fe: Bear & Co., 1982.

Kopp, Sheldon B. *Guru*. Palo Alto: Science and Behavior Books, 1971.

Lawrence, D. H. *Selected Poems*. New York: Viking Press, 1959.

Leech, Kenneth L. *Spirituality and Pastoral Care*. Boston: Cowley Publications, 1990.

Merton, Thomas. *New Seeds of Contemplation*. New York: New Directions, 1962.

Monique, Eugene. *Phallos, The Sacred Image of the Masculine*. Toronto: Inner City Books, 1987.

Nouwen, Henri J. *The Way of the Heart*. San Francisco: Harper-Collins, 1981.

Oliver, Mary. *American Primitive*. Boston: Little, Brown, 1983.

Pennington, M. Basil. *The Monastic Way.* New York: Crossroad Publishing Company, 1980.

———. *Thomas Merton, Brother Monk.* New York: Harper & Row, 1987.

Ross, Maggie. *Pillars of Flame.* New York: Harper & Row, 1988.

Sanford, John. *Healing and Wholeness.* New York: Paulist Press, 1977.

Shannon, William H. *Silence On Fire.* New York: Crossroad Publishing Company, 1991.

Strong, James. *Strong's Exhaustive Concordance of the Bible.* New York: Abingdon Press, 1974.